COMMON ENEMIES

Their Uses and Abuses

John Douglas Peters

TP Treasure Press

COMMON ENEMIES

Their Uses and Abuses

Copyright © 2025 by Treasure Press
All Rights Reserved
ISBN 978-0-9915635-5-5

Published by Treasure Press, 418 Main St., Belleville, MI 48111
(734) 699-7784 • treasurepressbelleville@gmail.com

Thanks

To Professor of History and Political Science, Robert B. Dishman (1918-2014) of the University of New Hampshire and to Wilbert (Bill) McKeachie (1921-2019), Professor of Psychology of the University of Michigan for serving as readers of my manuscript.

To Christine Consales, Paul Cooney and Beth Dusevic for their invaluable help in producing this book.

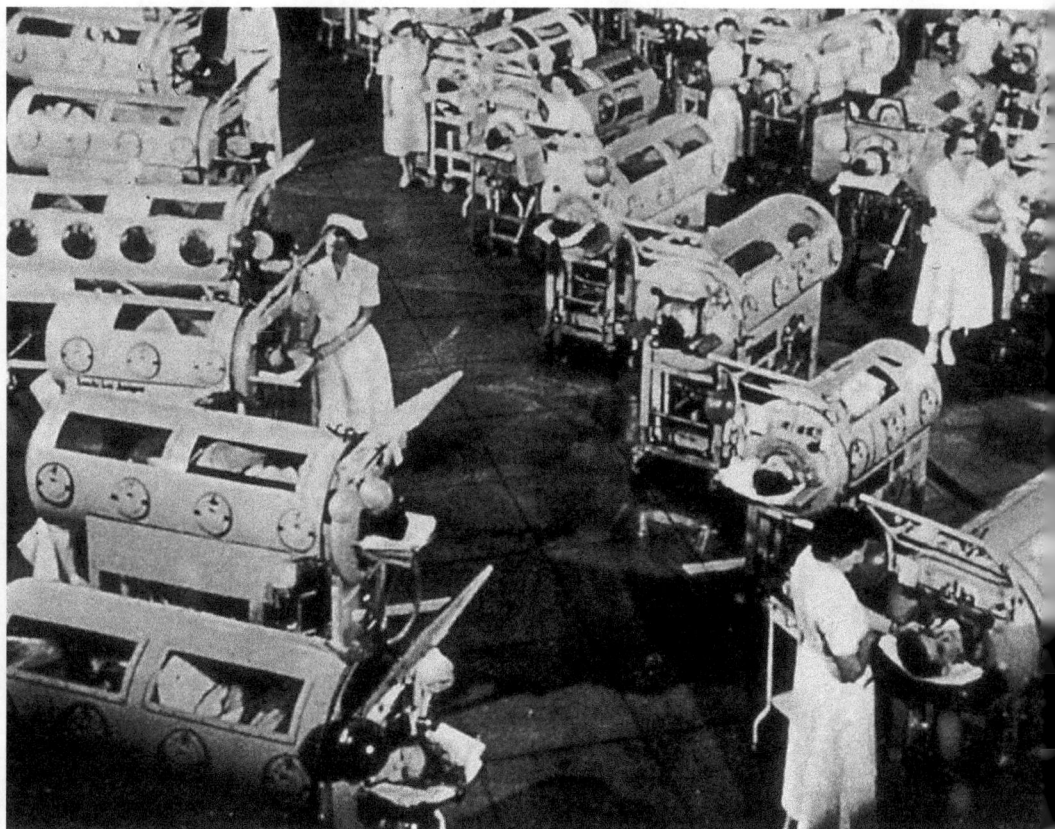

Many polio victims who lived in iron lungs could come out for short periods. Otherwise they lived out their lives in them. If the diaphragm and muscles between the ribs were fully paralyzed, the polio victim would be stuck in the iron lung for life. It would take two attendants to help the patient use a bedpan.

Polio victims would be limited to a view of the ceiling for the rest of their lives as the machine would take care of breathing for them.

Until vaccines were developed in the 1950s, polio was a Common Enemy bringing death, paralysis and disability to thousands. In 1938 President Franklin D. Roosevelt, comedian Eddie Cantor and others created the March of Dimes charity to raise money to fund the development of polio vaccines. Photograph courtesy of the Centers of Disease Control and Prevention.

Contents

Illustrations

Common Enemies are everywhere. There are big ones (nuclear extinction), close ones (the taxman), far-off ones (the federal deficit), immediate ones (cancer and heart disease), little ones (body odor and bad breath), cosmic ones (asteroids) and spiritual ones (sin, the devil and the religions that exist to fight them).

SECTION I

CHAPTER ONE

Introduction

Introduction

Although significant global events have occurred in the 16 years since the first edition of this book, including Covid, the war in Ukraine, Artificial Intelligence and tensions with China, none of these events materially change the analyses presented in the first edition. Rather, they add examples to the various uses and abuses of Common Enemies presented in the first edition.

Putin's war on Ukraine uses a number of Common Enemy tools. First, to mobilize and unify the Russian people he warns of the threat the North Atlantic Treaty Organization (NATO) poses to Russia's survival. He further mobilizes and unites his people by declaring that Ukraine is not a country, that it is run by Nazis, a recycled Common Enemy from World War II, and of course behind it all is the United States of America, a Common Enemy country that seeks to rule the world.

Covid presents a slightly different example. As with tuberculosis and polio, Covid should have been a clear-cut common enemy. Unfortunately for the world's response, existing political polarization in the United States caused a debate as to whether Covid was a real Common Enemy. One side said Covid was a virulent killer with no known treatment. The other side declared that Covid was no worse than the flu or a bad common cold.

The wearing or not wearing a mask became a political flash point. As with any new disease emerging science may reach conclusions and findings that change over time as does the significance of these findings. If treatments had not been found and if the death toll had not decreased, one would hope that the denier group would come around to the benefit of wearing a face mask as the science of Covid transmission firmed up. However, as we know, positions often become fixed, even in the face of overwhelming evidence. On the other hand, if untreated Covid evolved into a greater killer, and the death toll skyrocketed, the increased degree of threat would ultimately, hopefully bring the deniers around to the benefits of masking.

Covid has shown us that where there is a disagreement as to whether something is a real and serious Common Enemy, there is likely to be a delayed, uncertain and ineffective response. Ironically, Covid has also shown us, that the power of a viral Common Enemy can be neutralized by a technological advance such as mRNA vaccines. Ironic is an appropriate characterization since many in our population now view mRNA vaccines as a Common Enemy of mankind.

Although Common Enemies drive much human behavior in our world, from global conflicts to office politics, the first edition of this book (2009) was the first to look at how humans have used and abused Common Enemies for both great and evil purposes.

Common Enemies have always been with us. Indeed, they brought us together. They help keep us together, and in the main, they are powers for good. The Darwinian imperative of survival, shows that humans depend on Common Enemies for evolutionary advancement. Common Enemies are the stimulus for the evolutionary responses that advance our species, if they don't destroy it.

Since the beginning of time, individuals, tribes, cultures, nations and other groups have built their groups by using Common Enemies to unify, bond and maintain their "group". The earliest humans formed groups for protection against natural Common Enemies like lions, tigers, bears and other humans. The creation of "society" and other evolutionary advances, including laws, were stimulated by the existence of both natural and conceptual Common Enemies. Think of the historically combative Greek city-states uniting to fight the invading Persians in 490 BCE. The end result of that Common Enemy threat was the uniting of previously combative city-states and the creation of Greece, one of the first modern democracies. Think, too, of how each of the great religions has been built, fighting Common Enemies like the Devil, evil and each other.

Common Enemies are everywhere. There are big ones (nuclear extinction), close ones (the taxman), far-off ones (the federal deficit), immediate ones (cancer and heart disease), little ones (body odor and bad breath), cosmic ones (asteroids) and spiritual ones (sin, the devil and the religions that exist to fight them).

Millions of dollars have been raised to fight Common Enemy diseases such as Polio, Cancer, Heart Disease and Muscular Dystrophy, etc. Salesmen bond with male buyers by sharing Common Enemy stories about how their wives spend money or mistreat them. All of these are positive uses of Common Enemies, even though the last may be ethically dodgy.

Labeling a group or an individual a Common Enemy, or Most

Wanted, draws our attention to that group, or to a single person. Such a label shines a spotlight. Think of Public Enemy No. 1 posters. A mugshot, lots and lots of eyes looking for today's John Dillinger, and soon the Common Enemy is caught and jailed or killed. After that, another bad guy is given the Common Enemy, or "Public Enemy No. 1" designation, and so on. Here the Common Enemy designation is used as a tool for a good purpose, unless you're a John Dillinger.

Hitler used Common Enemies more skillfully than most. He unified his people by declaring Jews, Gypsies, homosexuals and social democrats Common Enemies and a threat to the Aryan gene pool. Aryan blood would be poisoned. After building fear, then anger and hate toward these Common Enemies, his followers (Nazis) stole their property and ultimately dehumanized these Common Enemies, such that otherwise sane people helped, or watched silently as Hitler and his followers exterminated millions of Germany's Jews and others. Hitler's plans were calculated, well-thought-out, intentional, but to most of us, evil.

Einstein believed, "We sometimes do things, but we do not know why we do them." If true, humans are capable of engaging in thoughtless acts. Genetic, emotional and unconscious factors may drive thoughtless, yet significant acts. Not all evil deeds come from evil intent. Thoughtless leaders can do equal harm by misusing Common Enemies. And real or perceived Common Enemies can drive leaders and their people into thoughtless acts. Sometimes groups of thoughtless people become a mob when confronted by a perceived Common Enemy.

When gathered into a mob, the danger of the mob engaging in thoughtless acts is great. Emotions and a lack of individual responsibility allow a mob to do what no one individual in the group would otherwise do. And because nothing can mobilize and unify individuals into a mob better than a Common Enemy, individuals must be able to recognize when Common Enemies are moving us toward becoming a *mob*.

Religions, it can be argued, respond to a host of Common Enemies. And these Common Enemies are the raisons d'être of these religions. The Devil and Sin are useful Common Enemies to all religions.

Sometimes religions fight for turf, or survival, by designating other religions a Common Enemy. Religions help each other out this way.

The Jewish Star, the recognized symbol of Jewish identity and Judaism, is known as the Star of David, after King David, the second King of the Israelites, who reigned about 3000 years ago. This star has flown on Israel's flag since its creation in 1948.

The Cross, a universally recognized Christian symbol, was used soon after the death of Christ. The written record shows its use in 211 CE. The cross symbolizes Christ's sacrifice for humankind. This symbol was also painted onto the tunics of knights leaving Europe to fight Islam in the Holy Land.

The Crescent Moon and Star is a universally recognized symbol of Islam. At the time of Muhammad (570-632 CE) the Muslim community did not have a symbol. Their armies and caravans carried solid color flags, usually of white, green, and black. Around 1454 CE, the Crescent Moon and Star was first linked to Islam when the symbol was adopted by the Muslim Ottoman Turks. Thereafter, a number of Muslim countries placed the symbol on their countries' flags. Graphics courtesy of Clipart Graphics.

Jews, Christians and Muslims have each, at one time or other, declared the other to be a Common Enemy of all humankind. During the course of three Christian Crusades, crusaders claimed that Islam posed a threat to the survival of Christianity and the civilized world. Remember the Crusades? Our Muslim brothers and sisters do. The religious persecutions during the Spanish Inquisition are another example of religious Common Enemy persecution. History shows too many examples of these conflicts between religion inspired Common Enemies and their victims.

Common Enemies can also be used to deflect attention away from a real problem. How many tin-pot despots have kept their people focused on an alleged Common Enemy, when the real problem was a disastrous domestic economy? North Korea is a good example. It uses America and South Korea as a Common Enemy to deflect attention away from its failing domestic policies.

Each of us is genetically hardwired to rise and fight a Common Enemy. As a matter of definition, Common Enemies pose a great threat to our common and individual survival. And if we believe Darwin, survival is a primal imperative. As such, Common Enemies drive the evolutionary process. Common Enemies, food and sex may be the pillars of evolution and survival.

By understanding the psychological triggers pulled by those using Common Enemies, as well as recognizing the signs of their abusive uses, we can avoid being manipulated into wrong thoughts, beliefs and actions when someone waves a Common Enemy flag in front of us. Hopefully this book will help us avoid the pitfalls of Common Enemy misuse.

On occasion we may want to point out a new Common Enemy to save our group; or to use or create a Common Enemy to achieve a positive use in our own lives. Thinking of FAT as a Common Enemy, may help each of us work to lose weight, or at least not gain too much more. What makes the study of Common Enemies so interesting is that it can take us from discussions of Hitler to weight loss in a few paragraphs.

People sometimes become leaders by their early identification, manipulation or creation of a Common Enemy. Consider American backbench Senator Joseph McCarthy who became powerful and famous for his discovery of, and attacks on Communists and fellow traveler Common Enemies who had allegedly infiltrated the United States Government and Hollywood in the 1950s. Exploiting the new medium, TV, Senator McCarthy rose to power by banging the Common Enemy drum, and fell to earth as he got caught over-inflating, if not fabricating, the dangers of American Communism.

Sometimes people can destroy a foe by declaring the innocent foe (scapegoat) guilty of causing a Common Enemy problem, such as economic recession. Individuals can also use Common Enemies to mobilize a movement to become powerful political leaders. Adolf Hitler labeled Jews a Common Enemy to racial purity. He also blamed them for Germany's economic crisis following World War I. In this case, Jews were a two-for-one. They were themselves a historical Common Enemy and scapegoat, and they allegedly brought on a second Common Enemy, economic depression (inflation). Two evils from one tribe of people, now that was amplification.

In the example of Hitler, he used Common Enemies as a tool for evil. Ultimately, his dehumanization of the Jews allowed average Germans to justify or passively condone the extermination of millions of Jews in the camps. Hitler's many and varied uses of "Common Enemies" could be a book in itself.

Also inherent in Hitler's use of Jews as Common Enemies was his recognition of the primal power of "tribes" as a unifying force, the Aryan tribe (agrarian) versus the Jewish tribe (urban). Hitler had a cruel genius for pulling the levers of primal human fears and emotions, leading to terrible and primal actions against an innocent people, all to advance the interests of Hitler and his tribe. These examples show some of the evil uses of Common Enemies.

At the other end of the spectrum, groups such as the American Heart Association and the Muscular Dystrophy Telethon, have raised hundreds of millions of dollars in the United States to fight Common Enemy diseases such as cancer, heart disease and muscular dystrophy.

Common Enemies can have large (World Wars), small (bad breath), and a range of consequences in between. They can have implications that range from the United Nations in New York, to the politics among the staff in a hospital or corporate office. Common enemies can be used, or abused in all levels of our lives, and among the lives of countries.

The many implications, phases, factors, quirks and legalities inherent in the use and abuse of Common Enemies suggest that this is an important topic. Surprisingly, to date, little research has been published on the many tactical and strategic options created by the use or abuse of Common Enemies. Hopefully, this little book will help change that. Common Enemies are too important a power to be so little studied and so little understood. Because money and human emotions can be abruptly moved by Common Enemies, we should learn as much about them as we can. Indeed, we ignore this subject at our peril. [1]

---

1. *There, I have just provoked an emotion in you by explicitly threatening peril if you do not learn more about the dangerous uses and abuses of Common Enemies by buying and reading this book.*

CHAPTER TWO

What Is A Common Enemy?

Defining Common Enemies

We all know what a "Common Enemy" is. We can give examples. But a simple definition is elusive.

Generally, a "Common Enemy" poses a threat to a group or to individuals in a group and can be something real like cancer, conceptual like the Devil, or it can be a manipulated fiction, like Hitler's Big Lie, that the Jews were Common Enemies, responsible for Germany's post World War I economic ills.

To be a "Common Enemy", a threat or harm must be perceived by a group. The common person in that group must perceive a risk and the danger.

The danger posed by a Common Enemy stimulates biological, as well as conscious and unconscious psychological responses in both the target of the Common Enemy (See Chapter 3) and the Common Enemy itself. In the target victim, from an evolutionary perspective, biological responses (adrenaline and other hormones) and neural reflexes, probably precede cognitive responses. But the survival or death of the target victim is a natural part of life's struggle for survival of the most fit individuals within the Common Enemy's target group.

Animals are genetically hardwired to respond to Common Enemies. To survive the attacks of Common Enemy predators, fish form schools, zebras form herds and humans form tribes, cities, states and nations. Possibly if confronted by an alien Common Enemy from space, we might even become the United Nations of Earth, and band together to fight the alien Common Enemy.

Common Enemies can be obvious; think of lions as Common Enemies of zebras and early humans. Or they can be tiny problems pulled from obscurity and marketed as Common Enemies; think body odor and bad breath, enemies that can only be combatted by the purchase of Right Guard deodorant and Colgate toothpaste.

Sometimes the Common Enemy of a group may simply be the opposite (Yin-Yang) of its Common Enemy; think of Communists and Capitalists. Indeed, there is frequently a Yin-Yang relationship between Common Enemies and their target victims. Absent genocide, Yin-Yang conflict between Common Enemy and target victim, or mutual Common Enemies, continues ad infinitum, unless one or both poop out, too tired to continue, or one destroys the other. Sometimes, too, a new Common Enemy will come along prompting previously competing Common Enemies to form an alliance against the new Common Enemy.

Examples of Popular "Common Enemies"

Sometimes we can define a multifaceted concept such as Common Enemies by presenting and discussing popular examples. You, the reader, can certainly add to this list, as popular Common Enemies are everywhere – large and small, and often in plain sight.

An overview of the many uses and abuses of Common Enemies becomes obvious as we look at popular Common Enemies. The Uses and Abuses of Common Enemies are more fully discussed in the following six chapters: Human Evolution

(Ch. 4); Mobilization, Unification and Maintenance of Groups (Ch. 5); Controlling and Manipulating Human Behavior (Ch. 6); To Scapegoat and Deflect Attention (Ch. 7); To Excuse or Justify Human Action or Inaction (Ch. 8); and, To Denigrate, Confiscate and Exterminate (Ch. 9).

Although each of these subjects get a chapter treatment later in this book, the list of popular Common Enemies that now follows, is presented in the framework of the following chapters.

Human Evolution and Natural Common Enemies

War, famine, disease, pestilence and *poverty* are Common Enemies to humankind. We know their names well. They have been our Common Enemies since the beginning of time, and they probably play a direct and positive role in human evolution. Lions, tigers, poisonous snakes and bears have also been natural Common Enemies since the dawn of man. These Common Enemies under Darwin's Theory take out the sick, the old and weak, genetically advancing the human species.

To Mobilize, Unify and Maintain a Group (tribe, race, religion or country, etc.)

Popular Common Enemies include:

1. *Jews* – Historically, Jews have been scapegoated and marketed as Common Enemies since the earliest civilizations, probably because they are one of the oldest groups with a consistently

defined identity, their monotheist religion and cultural characteristics. And until 1948, they were a people without a land. Ironically, constant bombardment as the Common Enemies of someone or the other, sustains their unity and solidarity. Hitler used them to build the Nazi party out of the ashes of WWI. His designation of Jews as the Common Enemy of the Aryan races was used to demonize them, to justify the confiscation of their property, and ultimately to cause otherwise sane people to participate in their extermination as the alleged final solution to Germany's problems. Iran's former President Ahmadinejad used Jews, the State of Israel, and America to deflect the attention of the Iranian people from his government's disastrous economic policies, and oppressive social policies.

Iranian President Mahmoud Ahmadinejad was born on October 28, 1956. Coming from a poor background, he earned a doctorate in civil engineering. Early in his political career he accused the United States of being against Islam. He supports the Palestinian cause, denies the Jewish Holocaust and thinks Israel should be destroyed. He and his government supporters have well-declared nuclear ambitions, for peaceful purposes they say. In this photograph by flickr, the Iranian President is lecturing at Columbia University in New York on September 24, 2007. Only the future will tell who is whose Common Enemy. Photograph courtesy of flickr and Columbia University.

2. *Christians* – Jesus Christ and His followers quickly became the Common Enemy of the established order. In Matthew, Chapter 22, the Pharisees and the Herodians united against Jesus. Even though they hated each other, they were united by their Common Enemy, Jesus. Ironically, the Roman response to Jesus, killing him by crucifixion, mobilized and ultimately defined Christianity. And the cross, the instrument of Jesus' death, has become The Christian Symbol.

3. *Muslims* – From the earliest days of Islam, when Mohammad left Mecca to ensure the safety of his followers, the established order in Mecca sent its army to exterminate Mohammad because he and his followers were perceived to be a Common Enemy threat to the established religious and political order. Ironically, Mohammad's underdog resistance to his more powerful Meccan Common Enemies drew Bedouin followers to his cause and this new monotheistic religion. Thus the little upstart Common Enemy (Mohammad) and Islam were made greater by their Common Enemy, the Meccan opposition. Upon his victory, Mohammad entered Mecca in 629 CE with his 10,000 strong Muslim army, and the rest is history.

Later in history, Christian Europe waged three crusades against Islam, the Common Enemy of Christianity. Once declared a Common Enemy, Christian Europe and its Knights felt justified in seizing loot and land. They got into such a righteous tizzy, they went on to sack Constantinople (Istanbul,

Turkey), a Christian city.

4. *Catholics* – After the Protestant Reformation, the upstart Protestants feeling persecuted by the Catholic Church, effectively mobilized and built their Christian sects by declaring Catholicism to be a Common Enemy. Discussing alleged Catholic intolerance in his Second Treatise, English political philosopher John Locke, called for uniting Protestants against (Catholics) this "Common Enemy".

5. *Communists* are the Common Enemy of Capitalists and vice versa. Each system tries to enhance and maintain itself by uniting its group by resisting the threat of the other and by trying to out compete each other.

Other Yin-Yang popular Common Enemies are: Arabs and Jews; the Rich and the Poor; Turks and Armenians; Environmentalists and Polluters; Settlers and Indians, etc. Each is the Common Enemy of the other. Whether true or not, each group perceives (or pretends to believe) that the other, is a mortal, monetary or theological threat to it. Each is mobilized, unified and maintained by its belief that the other group is its Common Enemy. Often, at stake is turf, or land and who will control it.

Controlling and Manipulating Human Behaviors

Human leaders commonly attempt to manipulate and control human behavior by declaring certain behaviors to be sins or Common Enemies of humankind. Examples include

1. The Seven Deadly Sins: *Greed* is bad, whereas generosity and sharing is a social good. *Lust* leads to the breakup of families and leads to social disorder. *Gluttony* is a sin because one individual, the glutton, eats too much of the group's food. Today, most would agree that gluttons get fat, develop diabetes, heart disease, etc. and use up too many of society's healthcare dollars. The United States Congress and several states are considering placing a tax on colas and other sugar water drinks, because they are unhealthy foods and will ultimately cause us all to pay more health care dollars. Congress also wants money to fund its projects. *Slothful* members of the group don't make a fair contribution to the group's work. *Wrath* leads to conflict, out of proportion responses and threatens society's peace and well-being. *Envy* leads to stealing, and *Pride* creates and wastes the group's resources.

2. The Devil and Sin are Common Enemies to all humankind. The Devil poses the ultimate threat. He wants to deny us everlasting life in heaven. He wants us to spend eternity in Hell. The Devil wants to steal our souls. Sin, the Devil's tool, shuts heaven's door to us.

The Devil is the personification of evil in various religions and cultures. It is the essence of an evil and destructive force. In Christianity the Devil is a fallen angel who is the primary opponent of God. In the Quran, Shaitan, also known as Iblis, is made of fire and incites humans to sin by infecting their minds with evil suggestions. In theistic Satanism, Satan is considered a god that is worshipped. Yin-Yang. Image by Inksyndrome@artwork on FreePik.

To avoid these Common Enemies, we must behave, that is, do not sin, and do not violate religious, social mores and folkways. Honor mothers and fathers, do not steal or commit adultery.... One religion laid down Ten Commandments to counter these Common Enemies, and many of the others say the same things in other words. These commandments are laws intended to promote societal peace and progress. They are intended to curb our baser instincts.

Frequently, conceptual and literal Common Enemies will be merged to enhance the threat of the conceptual Common Enemy. For example, the Devil is easier to understand when it takes on the form of a snake, as it does in the story of Adam and Eve. And on the flip side, we have seen Jews made to look evil when they are illustrated as having glaring red eyes, hooked noses and menacing ears that evoke the appearance of the Devil. The joining of conceptual and literal Common Enemies exceeds the power and threat of each individually.

3. Behaviors such as overeating leading to being grossly overweight, alcoholism, drug addiction or murderous acts are destructive societal problems that have been declared Common Enemies. Society wants to discourage human behaviors that lead to being fat, drunk or stoned. These societal behaviors are proscribed to prevent drunk driving deaths, drug related thefts, murders and other events that are disruptive and costly to our society. This class of Common Enemies also has a Yin-Yang counterpart. Although no one argues that being fat, drunk or stoned is generally beneficial

to the group. General Mills, Budweiser, the Sackler family and the entertainment industry promote the food products, drugs and behaviors that cause obesity (think chips), alcoholism and drug use. Those who violate serious behavioral laws like murderers, rapists and armed robbers are called pirates, outlaws and criminals. They become, by their acts, Common Enemies of society. From the time they are declared Common Enemies (Public Enemy No. 1) they are hunted, captured, imprisoned and their property seized. Sometimes they are killed.

To Excuse or Justify Human Behaviors

Terrorist suicide bombers feel justified blowing up thousands of innocent victims because they are fighting a Common Enemy, such as the Great Satan, the United States of America.

In America's Yin-Yang relationship with Al-Qaeda, Al-Qaeda's atrocity against the United States made Al-Qaeda America's number one Common Enemy overnight. Until September 11, 2001, few, if any, Americans had ever heard of Al-Qaeda. Nonetheless, for some time before September 11, 2001, Al-Qaeda and its leader, Bin Laden, had viewed the United States as a Common Enemy threat to the survival of Saudi religion and culture because American soldiers were stationed in Saudi Arabia, although it was at that country's request.

From a public relations and marketing perspective in the Muslim world, the evil of the United States is enhanced by linking the literal (the United States) and conceptual Common Enemies (the Devil, the Great Satan). Unfortunately, shortly thereafter, United States President George W. Bush declared that the United States was at war (sic Crusade) against radical Islam. And now that the United States was at war against a Common Enemy, radical Islam, the United States had justification to attack Saddam Hussein and Iraq. Huh?

By transferring the wrong of Al-Qaeda to Iraq, Iraq became the reverse of the old Arab adage, the enemy of my enemy is my friend. Or as President Bush might have said, the friend of my enemy is my enemy. It later turned out that Iraq and Al-Qaeda were not friends, as United States Vice President Cheney later admitted to the American people. Oh well. The power of a Common Enemy misused.

Leaders who abuse and misuse Common Enemies seem to do poorly in history while leaders who fight real Common Enemies, without pretense, and where true survival is at issue, often enter the pantheon of great leaders. Think of U.S. President Franklin D. Roosevelt fighting Hitler and polio.

Immigrants are a popular Common Enemy, especially during hard economic times. Immigrants allegedly take our jobs and use expensive social services. Once designated Common Enemies by a large segment of the United States population, legislatures and governmental agencies have license to do legal, illegal and stupid things.

The fence being built and snaking along America's southern border, is one of these responses. All the experts say that billion dollar fences won't keep immigrants from crossing over, under and around the United States' southwestern border. Yet it is being built to make Americans feel protected from this alleged invading immigrant army of criminals and drug smugglers.

Sometimes the appearance of action against a Common Enemy buys leaders time to figure out something that might work, or at least stall for time until the problem Common Enemy becomes a successor's problem.

The popular Common Enemies listed above are also useful in Creating Scapegoats, Deflecting Attention and as Justification for Confiscation of Property and Land. Many of the popular Common Enemies listed above have been denigrated to the point of iconic stature. Think Jews, Muslims, Gypsies, Australian Aborigines, American Indians, immigrants and on and on.

However defined and however used, Common Enemies, real or fictional, are powerful drivers of individual and group behaviors. Often, Common Enemies define themselves and their target group. Their conflict rather than their other accomplishments define them. Their battles become epics and the players become history. Common Enemies can be forces for either good or evil or both, but they are always powerful forces.

This definitional review of popular and frequently used Common Enemies is presented to stimulate readers to think of other popular Common Enemies we know and to think of less popular Common Enemies that are nonetheless important to each of us in our daily lives.

CHAPTER THREE

The Psychology of Common Enemies

A number of psychological dynamics are involved in an individual's (or group's) recognition of, and response to, Common Enemies and the fear they generate.

A Common Enemy poses a danger (stimulus), and an individual or group senses this danger through the senses of sight, sound, smell, feel or taste. Reflex or habitual survival responses (response) may be immediate. Concurrently, biological changes hit the individual, causing the endocrine system to crank out adrenaline and other drugs that stimulate the primal fight or flight response. Adrenaline heightens the senses and stimulates the brain, increases heart rate and causes a surge in energy.

At some point the cognitive part of the brain fires up and the "facts" gathered by the senses are processed and evaluated after the initial emotional reflex response. Then a cognitive response, or non-response, is made to the Common Enemy threat. Unless, of course, a reflex response has already lead to action, and that action has already changed the equation, requiring more cognition.

Sometimes there is no time or desire for cognition. In such a climate, one who advocates patience and reason might become a Common Enemy of the mob.

When given time to determine whether someone or something is really a Common Enemy, and when given time to identify a proportional response, the danger of taking a wrong or counter-productive action is less. Such a deliberative process is usually the result of experience, training, discipline, good information, good leadership and sometimes plain old "good luck".

The greatest danger may come from false and/or fast-changing facts, and having no-time-to-think. Are those blips on the radar screen artifact or incoming nuclear missiles?

Training and discipline can prepare humans to control their first and primal reflex responses. Training and experience can also imprint habitual responses. War games and other forms of training teach us how to rationally respond to Common Enemy scenarios before they happen. That is why militaries use war games as part of their training package.

Common Enemies threaten the survival of individuals and the group. From an evolutionary perspective, the survival of the fittest causes individuals and their groups to adapt and evolve in response to Common Enemies that kill the weak, the sick, the stupid and the unlucky. In his discussion on evolution, Friedrich Nietzsche coined the pointed observation that the enemy "which doesn't kill us makes us stronger", thereby advancing the individual and the species.

Psychological concepts crucial to an understanding of how humans perceive and respond to Common Enemies include:

1. human bonding
   -survival bonding
   -affectional bonding
   -opportunistic bonding

2. stimulus-response (s-r), where the Common Enemy is the stimulus and the responses are:
   -fear
   -anger
   -hate
   -defense
   -attack

3. nature v. nurture
   -learning
   -motivation
   -action
   -figural aftereffect
   -stimulus generalization
   -Common Enemy phobia
   -systematic desensitization

Common Enemies, for reasons we now explore, create some of the strongest human bonds and group unity.

1. Human bonding promotes evolutionary survival. Babies bond to their mothers through breastfeeding, and the mutual support family members provide each other strengthens the family bond and enhances a family's chances for survival. The extended family then becomes the building block of the tribe.

   Psychologists have published many studies on maternal, family, marriage and kinship bonding. But little has been published on non-family group bonding. One obvious exception is the "Band of Brothers" who fight enemies in wars. Surprising, too, is that little was published before 2009 on the ways Common Enemies can be used to bond groups and manipulate human behavior.

   Motivations for individual and group bonding include:

   Survival and Security Bonding. Included here are issues of evolutionary survival. The first tribes were bound by blood. Ensuring the survival of a bloodline is a primal imperative. Traumatic bonding occurs when individuals or groups are stressed by extreme and prolonged danger. Think of people lost at sea in a lifeboat.

   Combat bonding brings individuals together, as in a Band of Brothers. The trauma of being in jail or in captivity also bonds, sometimes strangely. Patty Hearst, kidnapped by the Symbionese Liberation Army, bonded with her captors, and converted from Patty the newspaper heiress to "Tania" the bank robber. Psychologists call this bonding the Stockholm syndrome.

When groups are traumatized, as was America and the world when Al-Qaeda sent kamikaze passenger planes into the Twin Towers of the World Trade Center and the Pentagon, a bond of fear, revulsion and revenge brought America together and most of the world together with America. This Common Enemy, this Al-Qaeda, bonded and unified America and most of the world as it declared its War on Terrorism.

Ultimately, the first purpose of Government is to protect the survival and security of its citizens. Without Common Enemies, libertarians would argue there would be no need for government. To libertarians, a common defense against Common Enemies is the only purpose of government.

Affectional Bonding includes love and emotional support: to be hugged; to be touched and groomed; to make love. Maternal/Paternal; Human; Animal; Spousal and Family bonding unifies and maintains all of our personal affiliations. These bonds are sealed by food, sex, mutual aid, contracts of marriage, body chemistry and blood.

There is evidence from the studies of various species that hormones such as Vasopressin and Oxytocin are factors in reproductive, pro-social behaviors and the bonding process. These two drugs have been shown to stimulate maternal behavior and pair bonding in laboratory animals. Studies also associate Oxytocin with higher levels of trust in laboratory studies on humans. Oxytocin has been called the "cuddle chemical" because it enhances trust and attachment.

Opportunistic Bonding brings together individuals to enhance their wealth, position, property and happiness. Sometimes, by making one bond, such as a poor Sicilian kid joining the Mob, money, position and property can be gained by a single act of bonding. In the old days, getting a job in the General Motors (GM) family meant a good life was guaranteed. A bond for life. For the General Motors Corporation family, unity and motivation was provided by their Common Enemies, Ford, Chrysler and "foreign imports". As time passed other Common Enemies appeared - - outsourcing of manufacturing jobs to Mexico and China, and rising healthcare and legacy costs. Sometimes, too many Common Enemies can actually destroy even the most unified and motivated family.

The first human bonds were male-female and family. Then maternal-infant; brother-sister; first cousins, and ultimately, you've got the first family. Male and female roles lead to the organized protection of the family, the gathering of food and the provision of nurture and affection.

As families extended, including outsider blood, tribes formed, all for the same reasons that brought families together. Survival and security were the prime benefits of the bond created by external Common Enemies. Whether these Common Enemies are animals from the jungle or other tribes, it doesn't matter.

As time passes, tribes become more broadly defined to include: guilds, religions, races.... Each tribe remains tight as long as its unity provides survival, security, affection and opportunity. The absence of any of these, or anything that threatens security, affection or opportunity becomes a Common Enemy to that tribe's survival.

Society and the State are the natural outgrowth of the first family. The state offers more extensive and robust protection against larger Common Enemies. The State can provide better social and health security from the Common Enemies of poverty and disease. The State can enhance commerce and prosperity by regulating and punishing individual behaviors that might threaten the group.

The Family, the Tribe, Society and the State are formed for a common purpose. These affiliations form over time. Some form over decades, centuries and millennia. After a lot of thought, after much trial and error, the state that evolves from this is largely predictable to both the citizens of the state and to outsiders.

Naturally, upheaval and unpredictability are always in the mix.

A *mob*, in contrast to the preceding groups, forms on the spot. It is usually emotionally charged and lacks the established pathways that exist in the Family, the Tribe and the State. A mob has no history. Individuals in a mob have no individual identity. Hence they feel no individual responsibility. By definition, a mob is a group that is capable of doing something quick, stupid and dangerous.

Otherwise sane, civilized and ordinary individuals became monsters when they act as a mob. In how many western movies have we seen a mob of ordinary townspeople rush the jail to seize an evil prisoner, to hang, without trial, only later to find out the guy was innocent. Usually this group has fear, anger and hate directed at their Common Enemy, the prisoner. Sometimes the town sheriff diffuses a mob with either an appeal to specific leaders of the mob for justice or uses the threat of a double-barreled shotgun or both. This is where the *law* comes in.

Law is the set of rules we make to keep us from being our nativistic selves. The law is the set of limits, or brakes we put in place to help us control the nativistic impulses within us. In that sense, law is like religion. The law serves to control the animal behaviors of humans.

Sigmund Freud believed that people in a crowd act differently than when they think individually.

Other theorists suggest that the anonymity provided by a mob causes individuals to believe they won't be held individually responsible for the acts of the mob. Mobs also convey and build a sense of group power or entitlement that allows the mob to make its own rules.

From a family to a mob, this discussion shows how external and internal Common Enemies are prime movers of groups. Common Enemies and the variables of fear, anger and hate play such an important role in our decisions and behaviors as individuals and as groups, we must learn how we can be manipulated, motivated and formed into coalitions and alliances by Common Enemies. We must also understand how the absence of a history with a Common Enemy can cause us to take wrong actions too quickly. With new Common Enemies, we have no past upon which to predict the future, and the lack of predictability increases the already high fear level.

We must always be wary of Common Enemy promoters. We should learn their motives, and we should independently determine whether the proffered Common Enemy is really a Common Enemy.

We must also recognize how we can create, identify and use Common Enemies to achieve great outcomes, such as when we went to war with and vanquished polio, a Common Enemy to all of mankind.

Polio was the most notorious communicable disease of the 20th Century until acquired immunodeficiency disease (AIDS) appeared in the early 1980s.

Polio was first described as a disease causing "debility of the lower extremities" in 1789 by British doctor Michael Underwood. In the United States in 1916, there was a large outbreak with over 9000 cases in New York City alone.

America's most famous polio victim, Franklin Delano Roosevelt, was left paralyzed from the waist down when he was infected in 1921. Everyone knew someone or of someone who had contracted this disease that left its victims sick, paralyzed, dead or even worse, condemned to living life in a large metal tube called an iron lung. The mental pictures of this disease were horrific. Among the worst were photographs of people lying in iron lung tubes and young boys and girls wearing metal braces that ran down their legs as they used crutches to take each painful step.

Making the fear of this Common Enemy even greater was the fact that no one knew what caused the disease. Or, who among us was to be the next victim.

Massive amounts of money was needed for research, for education and for the care of polio victims. War against this Common Enemy was declared.

At this time, Medicine was only beginning to understand viruses and antivirals. The best optical microscopes before the 1930s could magnify up to 2000 times. Bacteria could be seen with such microscopes. Until the 1930s, no one had ever seen a virus, and polio was caused by a virus.

Electron microscopes, developed by German scientists in the 1930s, allowed medicine to see a virus for the first time.

In 1938 singer Eddie Cantor coined the name "March of Dimes" to ask Americans to contribute their dimes to fight polio. He told Americans to send their change to Mrs. Roosevelt, the wife of the polio-paralyzed United States President, Franklin D. Roosevelt. In spite of these efforts, the number of victims increased, and still, no one knew what treatment or precautions to take.

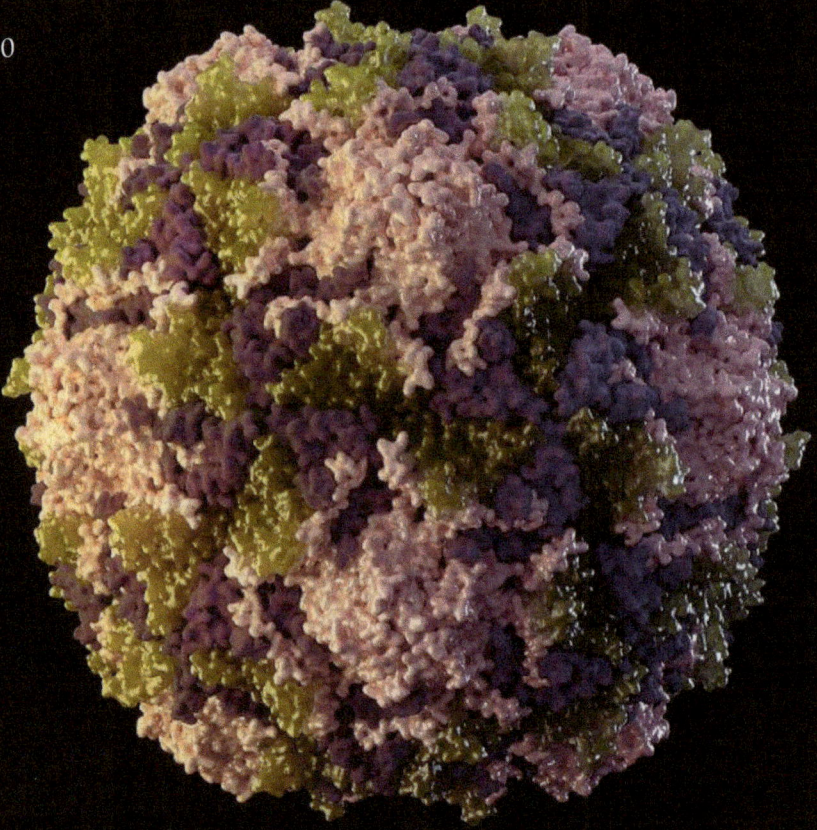

Viruses are raw genetic material, with a protein coating. They cause harm when they attach themselves to healthy cells and inject their genetic material into those cells. Eventually, the accumulating viral cells cause the host cell to rupture, which spreads out large numbers of viruses to repeat and amplify this cycle of destructive infection. The polio virus attacks nerve cells in the brain and spinal cord, causing paralysis in 1 in 200 cases. Although vaccines have eradicated this disease in most of the world, 90% of the remaining endemic disease today is found in India, Nigeria and Pakistan. The polio virus' shell, or capsid, measures 28-30 nm. Photograph courtesy of the Centers for Disease Control and Prevention.

In 1952 there were 58,000 polio cases in America, and in 1953 there were 35,000. Some cases resulted in death, but many resulted in life-long paralysis. During these years, there was hysteria as the disease frequently attacked the young. The horrors of polio were symbolized by the legions of children in metal leg braces or lying on their backs in iron lung machines. Nothing threatens the survival of our species more than attacks on our children.

This Common Enemy disease brought a nation of parents and their children together to make war against this Common Enemy. Dimes were raised and mailed, medical research produced the new science of virology (the study of viruses), vaccine science advanced, and electron microscopes and other technologies proliferated. This Common Enemy made us evolve to survive.

On April 12, 1955 it was announced that Dr. Jonas Salk, using March of Dimes donations from millions of Americans, had developed a vaccine to prevent polio. Dr. Albert Sabin's follow-up oral vaccine worked with Dr. Salk's injectable vaccine to seemingly vanquish this viral Common Enemy.

Unfortunately, there is more to the polio story. Polio still percolates in third world communities where vaccinations are spotty. Ironically, one of these communities in Africa is now believed to be the source of a newer viral Common Enemy, AIDS. And thanks to modern singer superstars like Elton John, our world mobilized to fight AIDS, a modern Common Enemy for modern humans.

When confronted by a Common Enemy, reflex-survival instincts respond first. Some of these reflex-responses are innate/hardwired, such as a baby's crying response to a loud noise. Some are also learned, as when we touch a stove's hot plate and get burned for the first time.

Evolution seems to carry with it both a need for and an aversion to Common Enemies. Our responses to Common Enemies often drive us forward as a species. Who doesn't remember the wars against tuberculosis, pneumonia, polio and other dread diseases? These wars led to great medical and scientific advances.

Common Enemies also stimulate us to fight, causing death and destruction. Are these two sides of the same coin? Or are they necessary steps in the march of evolution? Is this evidence that Nietzsche saw this when he wrote, "That which doesn't kill us, makes us stronger"?

Behaviorists tell us that much human behavior is a response to stimuli. Kick me and I'll cry out. This is a classical stimulus response (s-r). Usually, we will counterattack a Common Enemy that attacks us first.

Sometimes we will preemptively attack because we fear the Common Enemy will soon, or at least inevitably attack us, or we attack first because we reach a breaking point after being subjected to high threat levels over a prolonged period of time.

2. Stimulus-response relationships are also called act expectancies or habits. Over time, members of a tribe develop

a list of friends and a list of enemies. Over time, new and young members of the tribe learn who the tribe's traditional "Common Enemies" are. Think Hutus and Tutsis. They learn responses to these Common Enemies that over time become habit, or ritual, and these programmed responses are tough to undo. With time and effort, although rarely, such habits between tribes can be undone, and the threats to each other as Common Enemies can be diminished. Think Irish Protestants and Catholics.

As Common Enemies become institutionalized and as responses to them become hardened and habitual, various subgroups and individuals develop numerous incentives and motivations to see that Common Enemy situation perpetuated. They want to maintain the status quo for whatever their motivations are: land, hate, greed, advancement, political power....

Where war between the "victim" and the "Common Enemy" becomes the norm, great amounts of money and power are spent, moved around and gathered. The gatherers, usually taking a cut, like this status quo. They invest heavily in maintaining that Common Enemy.

Fear is a primal emotion, as are joy, grief and anger. Although painful, fear is a human survival mechanism.

Fear is a biological and psychological response to danger. Fear gets our attention focused on finding a solution to a problem. Fear is a component of survival. Common

Enemies, like nothing else, provoke fear and focus our attention.

Fear provokes physiological changes such as sweating, trembling, rapid heart rate and rapid breathing. Over time, a constant state of fear can cause severe psychological consequences. Combat fatigue affects soldiers facing daily danger over a period of time. The longer the time soldiers are exposed to danger and fear, more are affected by combat fatigue, a condition now called Post Traumatic Stress Disorder (PTSD).

Fear appears in human infants at about seven months of age. Young children generally have fewer fears than their learned and experienced elders. Possibly because they know so little of the real world, their ignorance denies them the tools (facts) needed to recognize and evaluate Common Enemies. They have fewer coping mechanisms, less experience and fewer problem-solving skills. Fear and ignorance are dangerous bedfellows. Because young children and the ignorant are the less fearful they are more likely to touch a hot stove. Once they get burned they know better. But when confronted by a new real danger, they are prime targets of Common Enemy manipulation.

In 2005, researchers from Harvard, Columbia and Rutgers Universities found the physical seat of fear in the brain.

It is located in a pea-sized area deep in the brain of all

mammals, from mice to lions and to humans. Inborn and learned fears are processed by an almond-shaped mass of gray matter called the amygdala. And within the amygdala is a gene that produces a protein known as "stathmin" a stimulant of fear and anxiety. These researchers have demonstrated that the protein stathmin is linked to brain circuits and registers both inborn alarm and acquired memories of fear. According to Vadim Bolshakov of Harvard Medical School, this protein is essential for survival. Memory of fear is easily established and is resistant to extinction and normally lasts a lifetime.

Although fear can be a powerful motivator, if it is too great it can paralyze. Think of the "deer in the headlights" phenomenon.

For fear to be used as a motivator in confronting a Common Enemy it should be modulated and accompanied by a plan of positive action to create a positive direction for the energy generated by the fear.

Tobacco products such as cigarettes, cigars, pipe tobacco, snuff and chaw hard tobacco, contain numerous human toxins and carcinogens. But they also contain nicotine, a drug that produces a euphoric state. Tobacco also reduces appetite and causes lung, mouth, stomach and colon cancers. Today, 20% of adult Americans continue to smoke, although this Common Enemy kills 400,000 Americans and accounts for approximately 20% of the American death rate. This Common Enemy, from outside us and within us, will continue to kill us for the foreseeable future. Photograph courtesy of FreePix.

In the early 1970s, using these principles, the American Lung Association and the American Heart Association targeted cigarettes as a Common Enemy. Real data proved that cigarettes cause lung cancer, and lung cancer kills mothers and fathers. These Associations and others taught school children to fear that cigarettes will kill their parents and make them orphans. Fear of loss and the threat of extinction. Each day kids would go home from school, begging their parents to quit smoking. Over time, this plan making cigarettes a Common Enemy helped reduce the number of American smokers. Higher taxes on cigarettes become a sellable idea as a consequence of cigarettes' Common Enemy status. The higher the taxes (cost), the lower the tobacco use.

Fear is both a response and a stimulus. It is a key mechanism of evolutionary survival. Fear is a pain, but it is life-saving. Fear fuels anger and even at a slight (stimulus), it fires hate, revenge and a response.

Anger is triggered by fear and frustration, such as when an individual or a group causes us grave injury, and we can't reach out and capture the offender, e.g., Bin Laden. The more frustrated we became in our attempts to capture Bin Laden, the more power he developed as a Common Enemy. As our frustration grew, so did our anger. Since writing the first edition of this book in 2009, Bin Laden was killed by U.S. Special Forces on May 2, 2011, almost 10 years after the September 11, 2001 Twin Towers attack in New York, NY.

Hate, for the injury done, and from the built-up frustration of not capturing Bin Laden, has made American hate larger. But when America allows hate into the room, cognition becomes clouded and reason is pushed aside. When this happens America is at risk of making a wrong or disproportionate response to a Common Enemy. Oops. America might have already done this. Think Iraq.

Professor Robert Steinberg investigated the role hate plays in terrorism, massacres and genocides. He concluded that hate shuts down cognition. It frees us from civilized human norms.

When hatred is amplified (by duration, frustration...) and directed against a Common Enemy, that enemy should expect no quarter. Even an innocent target victim must, at this point, become the counter-attacking Common Enemy of the instigating Common Enemy, in order to survive. This is war. This is when America, a self-styled "good guy", tortured its Muslim Al-Qaeda prisoners in Cuba.

Adrenaline flows through the veins of leaders during the run-up to war. Because some leaders may benefit from this, we must closely scrutinize the motives of those who rush us into battle against a Common Enemy. Adrenaline aside, we must also scrutinize those who make war for pride, for deflection, for gain or for other unjust reasons. The power of Common Enemies to mobilize us in a short period of time creates opportunities for mortal mischief by manipulative, ambitious, stupid or vengeful leaders.

When Common Enemies counterbalance each other and it appears that stasis results, frustration and anxiety may nonetheless increase. A small pin prick pain over a long period of time can become a very annoying pain. If frustration grows, anxiety may lead to anger, and the cycle of these two Common Enemies is accelerated. This increases the risk of conflict.

The multiple permutations of Common Enemies, their Common Enemies and innocent third parties cast in the role of Common Enemy target/victims, who in turn become the Common Enemies of the instigating Common Enemies, are infinite.

Real, falsely built on a scapegoat or created out of whole cloth, Common Enemies pose a multitude of psychological questions and avenues for research.

Such a question is whether Common Enemies and our responses to them are the result of Nature, Nurture or both.

3.   Nature and Nurture are two forces of life. Nature looks at what we arrive with at birth, and Nurture looks at what we learn along the way.

Common Enemies provoke instinctual responses, learned responses and sometimes responses that are a combination of the two. Some human responses to Common Enemies (e.g., snakes) are more inherited and hardwired into the human psyche than others, such as our long slow recognition of global warming/climate change as a Common Enemy. To young children, all snakes are seen as Common Enemies. As we age, we gain experience and learn that only snakes with red, yellow and black color bands, or snakes that rattle, are real Common Enemies.

Hardwired Common Enemies and Enemies that have attacked us in the past are an easier public sell than cognitively learned new Common Enemies. Environmentalists, for example, have raised and spent millions of dollars trying to educate and convince humans that global warming is a Common Enemy to all humans on earth, to little avail. To fight global warming is a much harder sell than counterattacking Japan after their attack on Pearl Harbor.

Finally, someone in the environmental movement has come up with a TV ad that warns us that global warming is a true Common Enemy. This ad touches our primal notion of species survival. Extinction scares us all. Survival is primal. The ad shows a mother polar bear and her cub stranded on a melting ice floe with no food as global warming melts the polar ice cap. Now we can clearly see that global warming is a Common Enemy to all of us because it threatens the survival of those cute, cuddly, white teddy bears and possibly our survival too. If those big, strong bears can be at risk, maybe humans should start paying attention to global warming/climate change.

Because of those starving polar bears, more of us are now bonded with environmentalists in a fight (money, time, votes, etc.) against global warming, our Common Enemy. Humans intuitively sense that if climate change can kill polar bears, humans could be next.

Learning. Although it takes longer to get "to action" in

response to a cognitively learned Common Enemy (global warming v. a snake) the response to a cognitively learned threat may be equal to or even greater and more sustained over time.

It's ironic, how powerful the advertising of Common Enemies can be. We all fear sharks more since the movie JAWS made sharks a Common Enemy. We now fear shark death more than snake-bite death. Yet sharks kill less than ten people a year around the world, whereas snakes kill more than 50,000 a year. How is it we've forgotten to fend off one of our "first" Common Enemies? Have we been deflected from snakes, a true danger, by Steven Spielberg's mechanical white shark?

Because most hardwired Common Enemies of humans are well known, and because they've been around for a long time, humans have developed and learned effective responses, e.g., avoidance and snake antivenom. Such responses may be less emotionally charged than the responses to new, cognitively learned Common Enemies. Humans may be more prone to making wrong responses to newly appearing and newly learned Common Enemies because of the emotional component, and the absence of comforting precedence or proven treatment solutions.

Preserving cultural-tribal identity thrives today, even though it relates back to small groups of primal humans and their evolutionary fight for survival against wolves, lions and tigers. There is an old Bedouin saying: "I am against my brother, my brother and I are against my cousin, my cousin and I are against the stranger."

As an example, if we put a stranger, a cousin and brothers in a boat at sea with short rations, biology suggests the family will dump the stranger overboard first. We see this every day in small to mid-sized businesses. When the owner's kid, fresh out of university, is brought into a well-established corporate management hierarchy as a Vice President, this Prince becomes a genetic threat to the non-blood executives. Some of the non-bloods may leave the company, some may stay and undermine, some may suck up, and some may continue to do their jobs to watch to see if the genetic Prince turns out to be a friend, foe, benign or washout.

Unfortunately, if things go badly for the company and its business, and layoffs and downsizing become necessary, the non-bloods, all other things being equal, will probably be the first to get tossed overboard. And if things keep getting worse, the cousins will have to go next. Indeed, external Common Enemies such as a shrinking market may cause us to lay off or abandon members of our own group if such acts increase the chances for company survival.

This Bedouin proverb shows the shape-shifting nature of Common Enemies due to factors such as inadequate food supplies. It also gives us an example of the powerful role Common Enemies play in human evolution, in the corporate hierarchy and much of the rest of the world. All other things being equal, remember the slogan, blood first.

Motivation is a science and an art studied and practiced by politicians, generals, coaches, parents and others, who want to charge us, load us up and fire us off at a target or goal. When Common Enemies appear, or are created, packaged and sold, our responses to these Common Enemies include fear, frustration, anger, hate, aggression and a fighting spirit. All of these human juices are extremely motivating.

Psychologist A.H. Maslow posited a hierarchy of motivations, with competence motives at the top; then self-esteem motives; then affiliation motives; and finally, at the base and foundation of the pyramid, survival and safety motives. Common Enemies that threaten the lowest hierarchy, must be immediately satisfied or they will become dominant.

Darwin's theory of evolution and survival of the species tells us that psychologist Maslow was probably right. Where starvation is the Common Enemy, in spite of laws (ethical luxuries), humans will and probably should steal bread to survive.

During the 1950s in America, the collective fear was that the Union of Soviet Socialist Republics (USSR), America's great Common Enemy, would rain nuclear missiles on American heads. Some Americans built fallout shelters to protect themselves from the nukes of their Common Enemy. Some shelter owners even admitted to keeping guns in their shelters to repel their hungry and shelter-less neighbors, as they only have enough food to ensure their own survival. Again, the shape-shifting nature of Common Enemies may be due to external variables. Today a friend and neighbor, but tomorrow after the nukes fall, our neighbors become our Common Enemies when they come to take our food.

A good Common Enemy rapidly and strongly motivates. For years, American scholars and taxpayers were motivated to fight Communism, America's Common Enemy. America went to Korea, Vietnam, Chile, Afghanistan and the Ukraine to stop Communism, a conceptual Common Enemy avoiding a direct and potentially more risky confrontation with a literal Common Enemy, the Russians. These surrogate conceptual Communist Common Enemies gave America a time and place to go to fight (Russia), the true Common Enemy. Proxy wars within a war often end with a poof, and not a bang. Think Vietnam and Afghanistan.

Because motivation, fueled by a Common Enemy, is a powerful force, leaders for good or bad, use Common Enemies to stimulate responses to real or fabricated Common Enemies.

Where one Common Enemy is so much greater in strength than its far-lesser Common Enemy, the latter may have anxiety (fear of attack) but it is nonetheless unlikely to attack its superior Common Enemy. Unless, of course, other friends of the little Common Enemy, or enemies of the large Common Enemy band together, setting aside their differences, coming together to fight their mutual Common Enemy.

Motivational forces shapeshift in the power fields generated by combat between Common Enemies.

Action or inaction may be the result of cognition and/ or hardwired processes. When stimulated by a Common

Enemy, either action or inaction may be an appropriate and proportionate response. The response may range from no action, a slight push-back, to an all-out attempt to destroy the Common Enemy once and for all. Even low intensity containment theorists expect, or hope that, ultimately, their contained Common Enemy will implode from within or just go away.

Action may be justified or it may not, depending on the facts. Is action taken as a response to an attack by the Common Enemy justified? Is action taken to preemptively seize a faux Common Enemy's goods, lands and lives justified? These are questions citizens must ask of themselves and their leaders.

Most humans do not like to think of themselves as bad people. Most of us would like to think we would never strike the first blow. For us to take hurtful or even mortal action against another, our psyches generally require that we be the defending victim, the good guy striking back.

For most of us to strike, we need to have suffered a real or perceived injury. Where there is a real mortal threat or a real injury from a real Common Enemy, few would challenge a mortal response.

The danger comes when greed, oil, land or other incentives color our decision to declare someone, some group or some nation a Common Enemy. Where the "enemy" is naught, but we want, we must make sure we are not creating a false danger, to justify seizing someone else's stuff.

Of course Machiavelli turns this around. He advises his

Prince to identify great lands. He then instructs the Prince to lead his people into the belief that the people of those great lands pose a covetous threat such as to make those people a Common Enemy to the Prince's people. War ensues and many die, but the Prince's people are victorious, and they now proudly possess those great lands. Long live the land-grabbing Prince.

Action is fueled by fear, anxiety, anger and hate. Depending on how the battle between Common Enemies turns out, the Common Enemies might end up in their original spots. Same fear, same anxiety, same anger. However, if it turns out otherwise, and one of the Common Enemies prevails over the other, and the other is destroyed, this would probably extinguish the conqueror's fear, anxiety and anger.

Action can have unforeseen consequences. In physical science we are taught that for each action there is an equal and opposite reaction. Although this may be true of swinging steel balls, it is not true of humans. The human brain is much less predictable than the elements of the Periodic Table.

Shaped by nature, and by nurture, coupled with an emotional soup of hormones, fear, anger and hate, human actions and responses can be varied, severe and/or disproportionate to Common Enemy provocations. Action enhances all risks, because action causes change. And with change, unknowns are created. But over time, the costs of inaction may outweigh the costs of more immediate action. Whether action works, and is proportional and just, is sometimes hard to calculate, even over time. Because of this, inaction is often the first response to our Common Enemy's threats. Unless a threat is as direct and blatant as the Japanese attack on Pearl Harbor was, more remote and less direct attacks often go unpunished or under-punished. Until Hitler invaded Poland, most of the world accepted his earlier illegal conquests.

The weapons available to a Common Enemy (nukes v. AK-47s) also predict action or inaction decisions. But this is common sense only up to a point. A well-motivated Common Enemy, even if only armed with AK-47s, can lead to big trouble. Think of the Vietcong and the United States' War in Vietnam.

To make sure Iran (and later the United States) would not attack his Iraq, Saddam Hussein rattled his saber at his enemies and boasted of his myriad weapons of mass destruction. His bluster backfired when the United States decided the presence of these weapons of mass destruction, in the hands of a crazy Common Enemy, was sufficient justification for America's first ever preemptive war.

Figural Aftereffect is a psychological response seen in humans who focus so intently on a form, such as a circle, that when they look across the page at a square figure, the sides of the square deform, and a circle is seen.

When humans experience fear, and focus intently on a Common Enemy, if and when they look over, to the next "Common Enemy", they may see their last Common Enemy. When confronted by a Common Enemy, and after periods of intense focus on that Common Enemy, we should think twice before making decisions regarding the next opponent we confront, to avoid making predictable mistakes due to the figural aftereffect phenomenon. We don't want to waste resources or risk injury fighting or fleeing a possible Common Enemy when all we are seeing is a cognitive reflection. Think here of the Taliban in Afghanistan after 9/11/2001, and Saddam in Iraq.

Stimulus Generalization occurs when humans respond to similar stimuli in the same way they were trained to respond to the original stimuli. For example, a small group of Saudi Arabs, calling themselves Al-Qaeda, became the Common Enemy of the West by blowing up the Twin Towers in New York. The world saw pictures of Bin Laden in his head wrap and flowing robes. He acted humble, yet sure. Much of the world hated him. When he struck America, America's first response was fear. Vice President Cheney went to an undisclosed location, just in case Al-Qaeda intended to kill all of America's leaders. Bin Laden was also a Muslim. America's second response was blind anger and action.

America's Prince, President George W. Bush, wanted to take on Iraq and Saddam Hussein from the onset of his presidency. Al-Qaeda, mankind's foremost Common Enemy after September 11, 2001, was hated and targeted for destruction. Iraq and Al-Qaeda, both Arabs and Muslims, and strangers to our culture, were one and the same, Vice President Cheney told us. Iraq and Al-Qaeda agents were seen meeting in a foreign country discussing terrorist acts. Iraq and Al-Qaeda were married by the Bush administration's public relations machine. This alleged marriage doomed Saddam, and ultimately, America's war in Iraq injured its reputation and cost it fortunes in lives and money. This might not have happened if the American media and the public had understood how easily third parties such as Saddam Hussein can be damned by leaders with agendas, who link a third party (Saddam) to a despised Common Enemy (Al-Qaeda).

Humans are vulnerable to the linking of innocent victims to real Common Enemies. One could argue that the American administration linked Iraq to Al-Qaeda's bombing of the World Trade Center. In this argument, Iraq was the innocent victim linked to Al-Qaeda, the generally accepted Common Enemy. It was a time of emotion and adrenaline. Although Saddam Hussein may have been guilty of many other wrongs, most authorities agree there was no evidence that Iraq played a role in Al-Qaeda's attack on New York's Twin Towers on September 11, 2001.

An early twentieth century experiment by psychologist John Watson demonstrated how this works.

> Watson first showed that his subject, a nine-month-old infant named Albert, had no original fear of a tame white rat; his response to the rat was mild curiosity. Watson had previously shown that loud noises elicit fear responses in young children, such as trembling and crying. In the experiment, just after the white rat

was presented to Albert, someone produced a loud, unpleasant sound behind Albert's head by striking a steel bar. After several such repetitions Albert began to cry and to show other manifestations of fear as soon as he saw the white rat in the absence of loud noises. (Watson and Raynor, 1920)

Like baby Albert, adult and otherwise smart people can mistake an innocent victim for a Common Enemy if the victim is linked to a real Common Enemy. Such linking is even easier where the victim is otherwise despised. Beware of loud noises and don't waste your time and emotional energy worrying about tame white rats.

Phobias, like Common Enemies, are driven by fear. Most people can handle fear to some degree. Some, however, are plagued by chronic and unrealistic fears. Sometimes these phobics blindly fear popular Common Enemies such as Blacks, Jews, cops or officers from the Department of Alcohol, Tobacco and Firearms (ATF). To some, often lone wolves, these Common Enemies must be fought, often in pseudo-heroic battles of right versus wrong. But as individuals can be phobic and wrong, so, too, can groups. Most Americans can now view the Ku Klux Klan as a wrong response to Blacks, who were the Common Enemies some Whites feared. Yet even today small but dedicated phobics persist in their fear and hatred of these popular Common Enemies. In stressed economic times, the numbers of phobics fearing popular Common Enemies increases rapidly. It is always nice to have someone to blame for our problems. Immigrants, cheap foreign labor, Blacks, women, affirmative action and "wokeness" are popular scapegoat Common Enemies during challenging times. Divisiveness is the handmaiden of Common Enemies.

Phobias resist reason. They come from a deep dark place, and they disrupt our lives. They make us both victims and victimizers.

When a phobic's cry against a Common Enemy becomes shrill, action against the perceived Common Enemy becomes more likely. Although psychic energy may wax and wane, a phobic's prolonged focus of hatred predicts some sort of action against the Common Enemy sooner or later. This is why groups such as the Anti-Defamation League and the American Civil Liberties Union are such important institutions in America.

Systemic Desensitization is a technique where the fearful or phobic person or group is gradually led through a series of exposures to the object of their fear. Consider the innate fear humans have of snakes. The first session may be spent talking about snakes. In the next session, the phobic looks at and handles pictures of different kinds of snakes. The next session, toy rubber snakes are passed around and handled. Eventually live snakes are brought in. Voila, another Common Enemy defanged.

History tells us the Greek city-states put aside their wars and animosity, where each city-state had previously been each other's Common Enemy for hundreds of years, to unite in 492 BCE, against the Persians, an invading Common Enemy. This example might be called, "Bigger, more alien and dangerous Common Enemies, a rapid desensitizer and unifier."

Although conflict and war may be inevitable, or even beneficial, maybe fewer conflicts and wars would be better. It might be nice to give it a try. It would also give many Common Enemies a much-deserved rest.

How many of our Common Enemies exist because we haven't figured out how to get rid of them? How many of our Common Enemy relationships continue because of simple stasis? How many of our Common Enemies are really Common Enemies? And how many of our Common Enemies exist because we want and need them? Yin needs Yang.

SECTION II USES AND ABUSES

CHAPTER FOUR

Role In Human Evolution

Spanking a newborn's bottom causes a reflex gasp that stimulates the baby to cry and take its first gulp of air. The doctor spanks to help. But to the newborn, the doctor is an enemy inflicting pain.

When humans first left the Garden of Eden, they came out as a family or a kinship group. Chances of survival were bleak. Wild animals, snakes, food shortages, disease, floods, fellow humans and other adversities became Common Enemies of all humans. Each enemy drove the behavior and stimulated advances in both the Common Enemy and the target group. Natural disasters which could not be factually understood became mythologized into religions or explained by constructs like the Devil, witches, evil and sin. Each, over time, has become a Common Enemy of humans. And over time, humans have evolved and survived in response to the real or perceived threats of their Common Enemies.

The Yin and Yang of Common Enemies was nailed by Jean-Paul Sartre in his play, *The Devil and the Good Lord*:

> ...to love one another is to hate a common enemy: I will
> thus espouse your hatred. I wanted Good: nonsense;
> on this earth and in these times, Good and Bad are
> inseparable: I accept to be evil in order to become good.

The human visceral response to Common Enemies is one of Darwinian survival. The response is chemically (hormonal) and emotionally amplified to ensure the strongest response to ensure individual or group survival. Ironically, never-ending conflict appears to be the price of survival and evolution.

Think of tuberculosis (TB), the White Plague, also called

consumption. Think about the millions of lives taken by this Common Enemy from the beginning of time up through the 1950's. There were a multitude of responses to this Common Enemy, including Shamanistic rites, quackery, patent medicines, quarantine and thoracic surgeries such as lung lobe removal. Many did little or no good, some helped. Ultimately antibiotics finally brought a cure. Along the way, medicine and surgery advanced, allowing later victims of other communicable diseases to benefit from what was learned in TB treatment. And as a Common Enemy, tuberculosis was beaten. At least for a time. This Common Enemy has now come back in an antibiotic-resistant form. Its original form festered and evolved in poor populations and countries. This gave TB a second act.

As an example, the story of TB shows how humans and tuberculosis have been each other's Common Enemy from the beginning of society. Each treatment has produced a counter-evolutionary adaptation. For a time, in the 1950s and 1960s in America, it looked as though antibiotics had defeated tuberculosis.

But tuberculosis evolved into an antibiotic resistant form. According to a 2021 World Health Organization (WHO) annual report, 10.6 million people were diagnosed with TB, and 1.6 million of these people died. If not for Covid infection deaths, the new TB would be the #1 disease killer of humans.

Can you imagine the spot the world would be in if it hadn't restrained this Common Enemy of humans? Life is a never-ending and evolving battle. As to any one individual, American country musician Hank Williams may have said it best, "No matter how I struggle and strive, I can't get out of this world alive." But we will keep on trying.

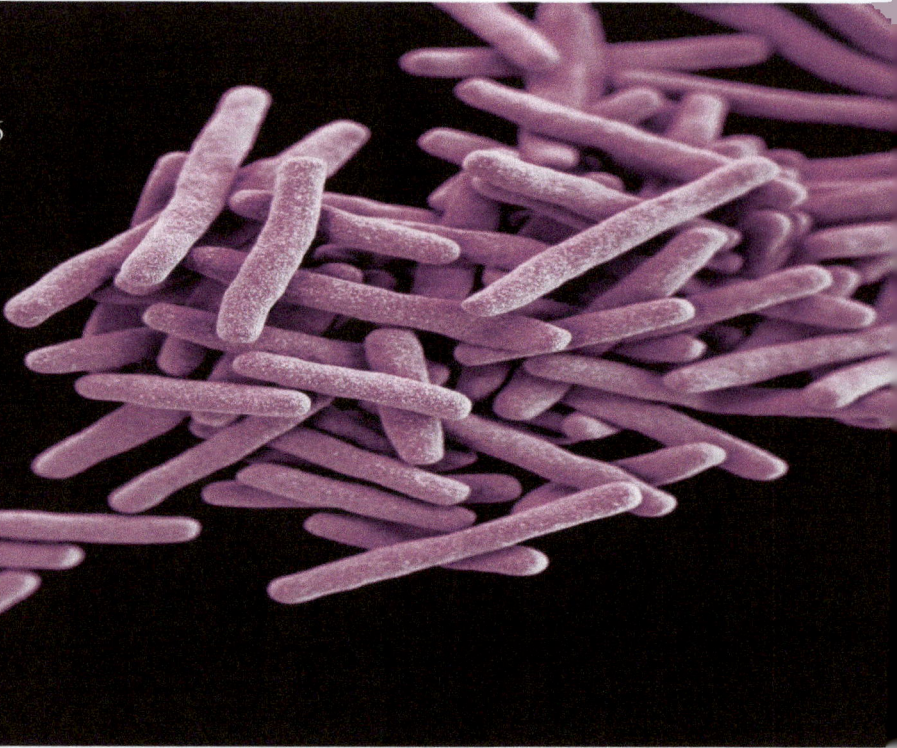

Tuberculosis is a contagious infection caused by breathing in the airborne bacteria, Mycobacterium tuberculosis. Although the bacteria usually attacks the lungs and causes slow and agonizing death by suffocation if left untreated, other organs such as the spine may also be targeted. In the 1800s, this disease caused more than 30% of all deaths in Europe. Although largely controlled in developed countries, WHO statistics from 2021 show 1.6 million deaths from this disease. This Common Enemy still reaps its human harvest. This bacteria ranges in size from submicron to 5 microns. Photograph courtesy of the Centers for Disease Control and Prevention.

This never-ending battle, according to Charles Darwin, is the essence of the evolutionary process. The evolutionary responses and adaptations to Common Enemies define a species' survival but cause great angst and damage along the way.

VICIOUS CYCLE

Pre-tribal humans lived in caves in small family groups. CEs from nature appear and threaten the survival of the family.	The threats of lions, tigers and bears reinforce the benefits of a tribe.	Humans become tribes to enhance chances of survival and to accommodate the expansion of their blood line. This, too, supports survival and evolutionary advance.	War and conflict with a CE is the endpoint of a CE relationship between CEs. Once victorious, the winning party needs to find a new CE.	For parties without a CE to bind them, disunity will follow. Hence, there is always a need for a new CE, or at least an old recycled CE.	Unity is maintained as the new or recycled CE must now be addressed.	In confronting this new or recycled CE the evolutionary cycle of life continues with conflict.

Research on predator-prey relationships suggests there is an evolutionary imperative, and a co-dependence. To an extent, Common Enemies and target victims have predator-prey relationships.

Theoretically, the smartest or best adapted mice and the smartest and best adapted hawks survive. As species, both evolve and continue, although many unlucky mice and hawks perish along the way.

When mice are plentiful, hawks proliferate. When mice are scarce, the hawk population declines. Although other variables such as disease and poisons (DDT) can effect these populations, the Yin and Yang of their survival is a form of co-dependency.

Common Enemies, whether people or bacteria, evolve in response to their evolving targets (victims of the Common Enemies). Evolution and natural selection continue to move, as the victim and Common Enemy become a perpetual motion machine. Unless one Common Enemy extinguishes the other, or unless both are extinguished by an external force of nature (e.g., an asteroid that hits the Mexican Yucatan and causes mass extinction), we can expect perpetual motion. We see, in the battle against tuberculosis, a Common Enemy's response to antibiotics, the emergence of an antibiotic-resistant strain and a persistence that shows how much tuberculosis bacteria want to survive. Even to bacteria, survival is the biologic imperative.

Society is also an evolutionary response to Common Enemies. Humans have organized families, tribes, societies to combat or defend against Common Enemies since Homo erectus first walked in Africa 2 million years ago.

In *Mutual Aid*, Peter Kropotkin suggests that animals need to assist each other in a struggle for survival, not so much as each against the other, but rather, as against the adversity of their environment. A hostile environment has always been a Common Enemy of humans and other life forms. If Kropotkin and former United States Presidential Candidate, Hillary Clinton are right, "it does take a village" to survive.

Whether following Kropotkin's advice or some other wisdom, our eyes show us that mutual aid, in response to Common Enemies, is the evolutionary mantra of families, tribes, societies and states.

If mutual aid is how a group responds to threats, the strength or proportionality of the response is the flip side of the same coin.

If we could apply physics to human behavior, we could hypothesize that cooperation among members of a group increases in direct proportion to the degree of threat posed by their Common Enemy. We also would predict, given time to think, that a proportionate response would have less blowback danger, and we would calculate accordingly. If individuals and groups were always rational, Newton's Third Law of Motion predicts that equal and opposite reactions would probably be seen. Alas, people and nature are in the mix, making unpredictability a predictable thing.

Individual and group responses are subject to great hereditary and experience variances in both individuals and in groups. We also know that irrational and monstrous acts may come from ordinary people when acting as part of a mob confronting a real or perceived Common Enemy. We also know many conflicts carry great emotional and historical baggage. These factors predict a lack of predictability and suggest the need for the education and training of citizens so that thoughtful responses can be made to both new and old Common Enemies.

Charles Darwin, the great English naturalist, was born on February 12, 1809, and died on April 19, 1882. He discovered and presented proofs that all species of life evolved over time from common ancestors. He described evolution as a process where successful mutations were rewarded by increased chances of survival. Survival of the fittest explicitly required an enemy to test and weed out the weak of the target species. This photographic portrait was probably made by Henry Maull and John Fox around 1859 when Darwin was 51 years old. Photograph courtesy of Wikipedia.

On the evolutionary road we travel, Common Enemies make us walk faster. They prompt us to invent cars, and now, the Common Enemy of climate change is forcing us to develop low carbon emission engines to power us safely forward down this evolutionary road. Should we be grateful for such Common Enemies?

CHAPTER FIVE

Mobilization, Unification and Maintenance of a Group

American social philosopher Eric Hoffer (1902-1983) tells us that, "Mass movements can rise and spread without belief in a god, but never without belief in a devil."

Parents, coaches, military commanders, presidents, scientists, office managers and each of us in our daily lives, try to motivate, mobilize and unify people. A danger, cast as a Common Enemy, is the most powerful tool available to light the fire, call out the fire crew and put out the fire for the common benefit of the group.

Mobilization: We and our leaders create or identify Common Enemies which are then used to mobilize, unify and maintain the various groups we belong to. The Lions Clubs organization, for example, fights the Common Enemy of blindness. Each year members of Lions Clubs across America mobilize their members, and outsiders, to raise money and to collect used eyeglasses, to fight blindness, a Common Enemy.

When the British fired on American colonial soldiers in Concord, Massachusetts, on April 19, 1775, at the start of the American Revolutionary War, the British unintentionally mobilized the Colonists by confirming and enhancing the public belief that England was their Common Enemy. The "shot heard round the world" also put an end to fence-sitting. From that point forward, you were either a Patriot or a Tory. There was no more comfortable middle ground.

Otto von Bismarck used the policy of *Kulturkampf*, a struggle for control of the culture, to mobilize and unify Germans in a common cause against the Catholic Church, which he declared was the Common Enemy of North Germans. He used this Common

Enemy strategy to mobilize and unify Germany. Ultimately, this unified Germany took on the world in WWI.

Adolf Hitler, von Bismarck's successor, watched von Bismarck's methods and later used the same Common Enemy ploy (Jews, non-Aryans) to unify Germany. Ultimately, this unified Germany took on the world in WWII. In the process this made Germany the Common Enemy of the world.

Any time a leader tries to build unity on false Common Enemy quicksands, people of all lands, not just Germans, should see "red flags". Bad actors can use a Common Enemy to manipulate us into bad causes and actions. We must recognize that each of us, and all of us, are vulnerable to siren calls.

On the other hand, putting Common Enemies to a good use, millions of volunteer "people's police" look for the FBI's Public Enemy No. 1. These enemies are bad, and we need to catch them quickly. They are Common Enemies and a threat to all of us. Here the villain gets a Public Enemy No. 1 designation. This paints a special target on the back of a single individual. For example, after the United States of America v. John Dillinger, America mobilized to finger John Dillinger, as a Common Enemy, aka, Public Enemy No. 1.

John Dillinger, one of America's most notorious bank robbers was born in Indianapolis, Indiana on June 22, 1903. His mother died in 1907, just before his fourth birthday. Robbing over two dozen banks, and killing several police officers, he and his gang became great newspaper fare and Public Enemies during the American depression. On July 22, 1934 he was shot through the back of his neck and killed by police. One more Common Enemy down. Photograph courtesy of the Journal Star.

Frank Loesch, Chairman of the Chicago Crime Commission, first popularized the term Public Enemy in the 1930s to call public attention to Al Capone and other Chicago gangsters who posed a danger to all of society.

J. Edgar Hoover and the FBI adopted the phrase to describe notorious fugitives such as Baby Face Nelson, Bonnie and Clyde, and John Dillinger.

Before Frank Loesch, the term Public Enemy, had been used for hundreds of years to describe pirates, outlaws and rebels.

Sometimes new Common Enemies are identified and declared to be extremely dangerous. For example, in the mid-1990s computer experts predicted that the business and financial worlds would be thrown into chaos because computers could not handle the transformation from the 1900s to the 2000s. This was labeled the great Y2K problem. Governments, businesses and individuals scrambled to find solutions to avoid the predicted catastrophe. This newly declared Common Enemy mobilized people and resources to address the problem. Many fixes were made and at midnight on January 1st, 2000, it turned out that the Y2K problem was a dud. The great Y2K problem proved to be a "nothing burger". Yet it may be that the Common Enemy declaration caused such a flurry of fixes that a real problem was actually averted.

In 2023 top Artificial Intelligence (AI) researchers and corporate officers warned humans against the "risk of extinction" in a 22-word statement. In that statement the scientists and professionals warned that "Mitigating the risk of extinction from AI should be a global priority alongside other societal scale risks such as pandemics and nuclear war." The ultimate fear is that machines and human life will be controlled by artificial intelligence, as opposed to humans controlling artificial intelligence. Whether or not AI is as mortally dangerous as suggested by the professionals' warnings will depend on how seriously government and industry take these warnings and respond.

Within weeks of the professionals' warnings about AI, various industry groups proposed plans of self-regulation to prevent against the harms predicted. Governmental agencies began working to identify regulations to prevent the harms predicted while allowing the many possible benefits of AI to be reaped. Thoughtful analysis and study of a Common Enemy's use and abuse potentials should always be undertaken. As the old cliché goes, "Don't throw the baby out with the bathwater."

Common and Public Enemies can be used to mobilize people for other good purposes. Cancer and heart disease are fearful killers. They are diseases that can kill us and our loved ones by the millions. By definition, these diseases are Common Enemies to all humans. We mobilize to fight these and other such diseases. We raise money, educate ourselves and fund medical research. Sometimes we make progress against these enemies, like polio, smallpox and tuberculosis. With heart disease and cancer, the mobilization and unity efforts continue, and they probably will continue until these life-threatening, old, lifelong Common Enemies are vanquished or significantly controlled.

Unification: In Matthew, Chapter 22, the Pharisees and the

Herodians united against Jesus. Even though they hated each other, Jesus was their Common Enemy.

Aristotle (384-322 BCE) observed that "a common danger (to survival) unites even the bitterest enemies." Common Enemies make strange bedfellows.

Theodor Herzl (1860-1904), the Father of modern political Zionism, wrote that "A nation is a historical group of men of recognizable cohesion, held together by a Common Enemy."

At one of their meetings, U. S. President Ronald Reagan mused to Soviet President Mikhail Gorbachev, "If only extraterrestrials were about to invade—then our two countries could unite against the Common Enemy."

Since Reagan's time, we haven't found any alien invaders but we have found the next best thing. On October 28, 2001, New York Times writer David Sanger wrote an article titled: "The World: Russia, China and the United States; In Terror, At Last a Common Enemy for the Big Three." They may not be space aliens, but terrorists are a great substitute.

From these few examples we can see that Jesus, Catholics, aliens and terrorists posed such a danger that otherwise hostile groups put aside past animosities to join in a fight for survival against their Common Enemy.

The mobilization phase is the most dangerous of the three: mobilization, unification and maintenance. Mobilization happens first when a Common Enemy appears. Often, mobilization happens first because a Common Enemy may appear suddenly. Sudden attacks, whether real or imagined, often provoke rapid and wrong responses. Remember the USS Maine? Do we remember the Gulf of Tonkin Resolution that led to a full-bore war in Vietnam?

The explosion of the USS Maine in Havana Harbor was taken by the United States as an attack by Spain on a United States ship, and hence an attack on the United States. That Spain was a Common Enemy was self-servingly touted by newspaper seller William Randolph Hearst. And, voila, the Spanish American War was on. In the Gulf of Tonkin, the North Vietnamese allegedly fired on a United States ship. By this alleged act, North Vietnam got the attention of a slumbering American public. North Vietnam became a Common Enemy overnight. America attacked, or counter-attacked depending on one's political view. In both cases no real attacks occurred. The USS Maine blew up from a coal dust explosion, and history shows it doubtful that Vietnam attacked a United States ship on the second day of tensions in the Gulf of Tonkin.

Two rushes to judgment. Two rushes to see Common Enemies; and two cases where vested interests identified and manipulated these new Common Enemies to create two wrong wars. One could argue that although the Spanish-American War was wrongful, it secured for the United States a major property acquisition. Think of Cuba, Guam and the Philippines. Could this have been someone's plan all along?

How and how quickly we mobilize and respond to old Common Enemies poses less risk of mistake than responding to new Common Enemies.

New Common Enemies create more fear as we have no past adversarial history upon which to base predictions of a Common Enemy's behavior. And because of this, the risk of making a wrong response is greater. There is no greater fear, than fear of a new unknown Common Enemy.

In conflicts between old Common Enemies, they have established mobilization and response histories, sometimes to the point of habit, a choreographed dance.

Old Common Enemies probably have a certain mobilization level already in place. The simpler and the more practiced the process, the less likelihood of making a mistake, and the lower the risks of misreading an enemy's actions or inaction.

When presented with a new Common Enemy, even when that Common Enemy is brought to us by a friend, we should be somewhat skeptical. The power of Common Enemies on us is so strong that both leaders and followers should think and think again before accepting and responding to a new Common Enemy.

The smaller the offense, the less likely the alleged wrongdoer is a true Common Enemy. Where the slight offenses are repeated often and over a long period of time there may be a real Common Enemy at work. The greater and more blatant the offense, think Pearl Harbor, the less chance an innocent actor will be labeled a Common Enemy.

Sometimes a new Common Enemy will appear rapidly, and time for thoughtful debate is short. Where the harm threatened is great, even to the point of survival, the fear of making an error must be put aside, and a prompt response must be made.

When the Greeks were attacked by the Persians, and the Spartans sacrificed themselves at Thermopylae in 480 BCE, the Greek city-states put aside their long-standing disputes and united to fight the Common Enemy Persians. The Muslim world, albeit based on a false promise of independence and self-determination, put aside its tribal disputes to unite against the Common Enemy Axis powers in WWI. Lawrence of Arabia gets much credit for using this tactic. The loot to be taken from this Ottoman Common Enemy was also a strong motivation.

Certain realities rob us of time and thoughtful choices, such as when a Common Enemy is suddenly and unexpectedly at the door. As English political philosopher Thomas Hobbes (1588-1679) observed in the Leviathan, his classic text on government, "...man by nature chooses the lesser evil." This is true, at least when man has time and the inclination toward thoughtful choice. There is also the problem of how to recognize and measure evil. With the Persians, however, their invading hordes were a case of clear and immediate danger. The Greek city-states had no choice, unite or die, the Persians are coming.

Not all Common Enemies are Japanese kamikaze dive bombers or invading Persians. Some Common Enemies are concepts or charismatic individuals that are not recognized as dangerous. On the surface and early on, these Common Enemies may present an amorphous, gauzy visage.

Great leaders and agents for change are often early to identify, market and use Common Enemies to spotlight and mobilize group responses to remote or conceptual Common Enemies.

Nelson Mandela is a perfect example of such a leader. In his February 25, 1990 "Address to Rally in Durban", Mandela knew he could not move forward toward a solution to apartheid until he mobilized two tribes with a history of significant conflict between them. To mobilize and unite these tribes, he told them:

> The parties to the conflict in Natal have disagreed about a great deal. We have reached a stage where none of the parties can be regarded as right or wrong. Each carries a painful legacy of the past few years. But both sides share a common enemy: the enemy is that of inadequate housing, forced removals, lack of resources as basic as that of water, and rising unemployment."

Mandela successfully built his coalition by showing the conflicting tribes that all of their peoples shared Common Enemies brought on by apartheid, and that apartheid was their true Common Enemy. He joined the conceptual to the literal. Food, housing and jobs were the literal, and apartheid was the conceptual Common Enemy, and these Common Enemies were one. Finally, apartheid in South Africa ended when Mandela's African National Congress (ANC) won the first multi-racial democratic elections in 1994.

Not all mobilizations turn out as well as Mandela's. Some, like the United States' declaration of war against Vietnam in the Gulf of Tonkin Resolution, turned out badly. The mobilization is often the easy part. Unfortunately, to maintain unity over time, the Common Enemy must be real, the cause must be just and the cost must be tolerable.

In a 2006 article on mind control, Internet author J.K. Ellis warned that, "Common Enemies unify, but what they sometimes create are mobs and some of the mentalities that come with mobs." Echoing this concern is an anonymous bard's observation that, "None of us is dumber than all of us."

Groups come together with emotions driven by a fear of real or perceived Common Enemies or problems. Where the Common Enemy is new and where vested interests are trying to push us toward action in a hurry, we should see red flags. Whenever someone says you must act immediately or it will be too late, stop and think. Who is the source of the recommended action? How immediate and great is the danger? What action is being proposed? What are the consequences of not acting immediately?

The risks of a "mob mentality" must always be recognized and assessed when evaluating a Common Enemy's threat and when developing a proportional response.

Maintenance of a Group: There must be a common purpose, and fighting one or more Common Enemies ensures a common purpose.

After the unified Greek city-states defeated the Common Enemy Persians, they recognized the benefits of unity. This unity enhanced commerce, reduced money wasted on wars between themselves, and besides, the Persians might come back.

Montserrat Guibernau, author of The Identity of Nations, wrote that:

> An essential strategy in the generation of a national identity consists of uniting people against a common

enemy. Since their foundational period, nation-states have been engaged almost continually in the fighting of war. Territorial, religious, ethnic, political and economic arguments have been employed to justify fighting against a wide range of external enemies.

Guibernau suggests that we must always have Common Enemies and perpetual war to maintain national unity.

Again, in the *Leviathan*, Hobbes wrote that,

...when there is no common enemy, they make warre upon each other, for their particular interests.

These thinkers suggest that war is inherent in man, and that for a nation to survive, it must have one or more Common Enemies (almost an excuse, see Chapter 7) against which our warring nature can be directed and our civilization advanced.

The German philosopher, G.W.F. Hegel (1770-1831) wrote that:

Perpetual peace is often advocated as an ideal to which humanity should strive. With that end in view, Kant proposed a league of monarchs to adjust differences between states...But the state is an individual, and individuality essentially implies negation. Hence even if a number of states make themselves into a family, this group as an individual must engineer an opposite and create a common enemy.

It isn't always nations that need Common Enemies to survive and thrive. In his classic political guide, The Prince, Niccolo Machiavelli (1469-1527) gives the new Prince this advice:

Without doubt princes become great when they

overcome difficulties and opposition, and therefore fortune, especially when it wants to render a new prince great, who has greater need of gaining a great reputation than a hereditary prince, raises up common enemies and compels him to undertake wars against them, so that he may have cause to overcome them, and thus climb up higher by means of that ladder which his enemies have brought him. There are many who think therefore that a wise prince ought, when he has the chance, *to foment astutely some enmity, so that by suppressing it he will augment his greatness.* (Emphasis added)

Machiavelli is advising the new Prince to advance himself by finding or creating, and then destroying real or cooked-up Common Enemies. If Charles Darwin was looking at this, he might see evidence of an evolutionary struggle for survival and dominance.

No matter who says what, if wars and genocide are end points of Common Enemies, we must beware of whoever points Common Enemies out to us when these Common Enemies are not otherwise clear to see. Often, too much is at stake for us to blindly buy into a Common Enemy. Impulse and fearsome dragons can lead us to folly.

The political philosopher, Hannah Arendt (1906-1975), in The Portable Hannah Arendt, discusses Rousseau and the concept of a Social Contract. She studies the agreements and circumstances that bind a people into a society. Arendt wrote that:

In Rousseau's construction, the nation need not wait

for an enemy to threaten its borders in order to rise 'like one man' and to bring about the union sacré; The oneness of the nation is guaranteed in so far as each citizen carries within himself the common enemy as well as the general interest which the common enemy brings into existence; for the common enemy is the particular interest or the particular will of each man. If only each particular man rises against himself in his particularity, he will be able to arouse in himself his own antagonist, the general will, and thus he will become a true citizen of the national body politic. For 'if one takes away from [all particular] wills the plusses and minuses that cancel one another, the general will remains the sum of the differences.' To partake in the body politic of the nation, each national must rise and remain in constant rebellion against himself.

If this is true, constant fear and angst appear to be the price we pay for the benefits of being members of a nation. We are both warriors and targets in our Common Enemy driven conflicts. We abhor Common Enemies, but they seem to spring from our essence and are necessary to our evolutionary survival.

One could argue that the key to Genghis Khan's (1162-1227) power was getting rival tribes to unite to fight and loot Common Enemies. Such an avaricious machine is hard to stop once started. This feared ruler attacked Common Enemies real and alleged and built the largest landmass empire in the history of civilization. Over time, there were fewer Common Enemies and no new lands to conquer.

By 1260, Khan's empire started to crack as wars of secession broke the empire into four states. Because they had run out of external Common Enemies, they warred inwardly and ultimately destroyed themselves. Again, history suggests that constant conflict and warfare are a necessary part of evolution. And to ensure that such conflicts are not directed inward, we must always have external Common Enemies.

Hopefully, there are positive alternatives to perpetual war and conflict with internal and external Common Enemies. Maybe lower threat Common Enemies can be used to maintain unity—e.g., low intensity warfare: war on drugs; war on poverty; war on crime. Certainly, with care and maintenance, we can keep and use these low intensity Common Enemies to hold us together. They are so important to our unity, we may not ever want to vanquish all of our Common Enemies.

In the past, the United States and other countries have directly, or through surrogates, maintained cold wars (low intensity) as well as hot wars (Korea, Vietnam, Iraq) often simultaneously, as they maintain national unity. In conceptual, or cold wars, we have skirmishes, incidents and diplomatic dustups, but usually very little or no bloodshed. Maybe, America and other proud countries should form a commission to identify low level internal and external Common Enemies that can be milked, like cows, to sustain each country's natural need for Common Enemy inspired cohesion. The use and abuse of these Common Enemies (Communists, Serbs, Armenians, Jews, Christians, the United

States, Russia and China, etc.) or each country's neighbors, can be monitored by an international group. Indeed, such groups were formed at the ends of both WWI and WWII. Think the League of Nations after WWI and the United Nations after WWII. Although some have criticized these international groups, they have helped us avoid hot wars, while they simultaneously referee cold wars.

Sometimes, even old, long-ago vanquished Common Enemies are recycled.

In May of 2009, Russian President Dmitry Medvedev, suggested that questioning the Soviet victory over the Nazis in WWII should be made a criminal offense.

Here, Medvedev uses the defeat of the Nazis, a legendary Common Enemy, to build a collective national identity for the disparate peoples who make up today's Russia. Thus, even though the Nazis are long-since dead, they are still serving a useful purpose.

In 2022 Russian President Vladimir Putin invaded the country of Ukraine as a continuation of his 2014 land grab of the Crimea. His justification for the invasion in 2022 was the threatening nature of the "Nazis" who control the Ukrainian government. This, although the Ukrainian president is Jewish. Putin resurrected an old Russian Common Enemy to facilitate his land grab of the Ukraine. Putin was able to sell his Ukrainian invasion by calling on the nationalistic instincts and memories of Nazi horrors to justify and build public support for his invasion. Putin also was careful not to call his invasion a war. He called it a Special Action. Apparently, the word "war" sets off too many "red flags" that would hinder his plan.

Although the principal use of Common Enemies is to mobilize, unify and maintain group cohesion, other uses are equally significant. Common Enemy strategies can also be used to manipulate broad ranges of human behavior, as we will see next.

CHAPTER SIX

Controlling and Manipulating Human Behavior

Enlightened kings, county commissioners, despots and city councils have sought to manipulate and control human behavior from the beginning of time. Early on, humans recognized defects in the nature of others and in themselves, but mostly in others. These sometimes dark natures pose a threat to both the individual and the group. To guard against these dark natures, these Common Enemies, we got Hammurabi's Code from 1750 BCE, the Ten Commandments, and now in America, federal and state statutes, regulations and local ordinances. Almost everywhere, we've got laws to protect us from our dark natures.

We've got laws, natural responses to Common Enemy behaviors, such as robbing, raping and killing that threaten the survival and security of our societies.

Manipulating our citizens, attacking enemies, catching criminals and interrogating terrorists are some of the many manipulative ways Common Enemies are used and abused.

Earlier in this book, American publisher William Randolph Hearst used his newspapers (the media) to gin up an American war against Spain by claiming that the USS Maine blew up from a Spanish attack. In reality, a coal dust explosion sank the Maine.

Newspapers, then radio, television, the Internet and other forms of media are often used to identify, attack and disempower Common Enemies. Sometimes, though, the media itself becomes a Common Enemy usually for the purpose of politicians who want their followers to discount and reject facts and activities of politicians who want to escape responsibility for their acts or to neuter possible critics.

In America today, for most conservatives, the media is populated by leftists, pushing leftist causes and being generally unfair to conservatives. To conservatives the media has become a common, unifying enemy of immense power. Former American president Donald Trump remains popular among conservatives because he is an avenging warrior against the New York Times, CNN, The Washington Post and every other mainstream (objective) media outlet. Former president Trump's continuing attacks on the media cause his followers to distrust, disregard and reject any criticism, no matter how just, of anything Mr. Trump does. As of 2023, he maintains a base of support (36% of Americans) by his continued use and abuse of Common Enemies. Mr. Trump is a superstar in his use of Common Enemies such as Muslims, immigrants, RINOS, the FBI, the United States Department of Justice and nasty women. Few people in the history of civilization have been as effective as Donald Trump in using Common Enemies to defend himself, to deflect the public's attention, to weaken and denigrate those who attack him, and in the case of immigrants, he rode them like a horse into the White House.

Donald Trump also uses Common Enemies to create sympathy for himself. He declares himself and his followers to be victims, innocent victims of their Common Enemy attackers. Playing the victimization card allows Mr. Trump to get two benefits from his Common Enemies. He unifies his followers and he gets a victim's sympathy for himself.

As to enemy combatants, assume American leaders in Iraq

want to stop the Sunnis and Shias from killing each other. Assume the Americans want to unify these two historical enemies into a new government that will last. To achieve this, the American occupation became the despised Common Enemy of both Sunnis and Shias, bringing them together against a Common Enemy, America. Although no one has said that America intended a Common Enemy manipulation, such a bonding between Sunni and Shia did occur, thanks to America's presence in their country.

In 2004, journalists Jonathan Steele and Roy McCarthy, of The Guardian, wrote the following headline: "Shia and Sunni Unite Against a Common Enemy, the United States Occupation." It would be nice to think that America was smart enough to intentionally project itself as a Common Enemy to unify the Sunni and Shia peoples. Who knows?

Albert Einstein observed that we do some things, but we do not know why we do them.

This is where advertisers come in.

Take human body odor, for example. It has troubled mankind from early times. After all, that's why perfume was invented. The worse the odor, the more perfume.

Over time, Madison Avenue has convinced us that body odor and bad breath are Common Enemies. So is sweat. To fight these Common Enemies, we mobilize and spend on gels, pastes, Lavoris mouthwash and Right Guard deodorant. We must fight these smells or we will be societal outcasts and die. Are we being educated, manipulated or both? And now advertisers tell us that pet odors and house odors are Common Enemies, too. The wars are interminable. Fortunately Glade and Febreze are there for us to vanquish these Common Enemy smells. Madison Avenue has a product to fight every Common Enemy, whether big or small, real or imagined. Or better stated, Madison Avenue will find a Common Enemy for products it is hired to sell.

A recognized advertising technique involves Demonizing the Enemy. In this technique, advertisers make people, with an opposing point of view, appear crazy, radical, socialist, communist... People with certain characteristics (fat) or certain ideas (Republicans or Democrats) are portrayed as Common Enemies. They are shunned, sometimes without, and sometimes with, justification.

Writer and advertising executive Brian Clark wrote an article, "Do You Have an Enemy? Here's Why You Need to Find One." In the article, Clark shows a salesman approach a potential customer. They chat, and the customer makes a comment about the expense of the item offered for sale but also mentions that his wife spends a lot on shopping. The salesman agrees that his wife also spends large amounts of money on shopping. At this point, the customer and the salesman have a Common Enemy—their wives. They bond, and a sale is made. Later, the savvy salesman admits he is single, but lied to benefit from the strong bonding power of Common Enemies.

Can warring groups be likewise manipulated by outside groups such as NATO? Serbs and Albanians bonded and united against NATO, their Common Enemy. Hypothetically, we can ask whether a group like NATO should intentionally mistreat Serbs and Albanians to turn them into Allies against NATO, so that NATO can achieve a strategic goal? Or maybe NATO's mere presence as an occupier makes it enough of a Common Enemy to bond otherwise warring internal factions.

An editorial by Mort Zuckerman, in United States News & World Reports, asks if "Israel [and] Arabs have a Common Enemy in a nuclear Iran." Wow, imagine Arabs and Jews coming together to confront a nuclear Iran. Imagine Israel is looking for allies to strengthen its position that a nuclear Iran cannot be allowed. This sounds like the prelude to a first-strike caper to take out Iran's nuclear facilities. One must remember to look carefully at the goals of friends trying to sell us Common Enemies.

Since the 2009 edition of this book, the United States has brokered the Abraham Accords bringing peace between certain Arab countries and Israel. A nuclear Iran, a Common Enemy, brought these formerly hostile countries together.

The United States Army recognizes the power of the Common Enemy tool. Its "Field Manual for Human Intelligence Collection", Chapter 8, quietly suggests that its interrogators:

> Operate within a framework of personal and culturally
> derived values. People tend to respond positively to
> individuals who display the same value system and
> negatively when their core values are challenged.

Bonding is the meaning of this message. Prisoners will spill the beans if they believe they and their interrogators have commonality. And nothing is more common than sharing a Common Enemy.

This is demonstrated by a few lines from a June 8, 2009 TIME article, where an American interrogator reports that:

> In the spring of 2006, he was interrogating a Sunni imam
> connected with al-Qaeda in Iraq, which was then run by
> al-Zarqawi. The imam had "blessed" suicide bombers.
> His first words to his interrogators were, "If I had a knife
> right now, I'd slit your throat." Asked why, the imam said
> the United States invasion had empowered Shi'ite thugs
> who had evicted his family from their home. Humiliated,
> he had turned to the insurgency. The American
> interrogator's response was to offer a personal apology:
> "Look, I'm an American, and I want to say how sorry
> I am that we made so many mistakes in your country.
> The imam broke down in tears. The apology undercut
> his motivation for hating Americans and allowed him
> to open up to his interrogator. The interrogator then
> nudged the conversation in a new direction, pointing
> out that Iraq and the United States had a common
> enemy: Iran. The two countries needed to cooperate
> in order to prevent Iraq from becoming supplicant
> to the Shi'ite mullahs in Tehran, a fear commonly
> expressed by Sunnis. Eventually the imam gave up the
> location of a safe house for suicide bombers: a raid on
> the house led to the capture of an al-Qaeda operative
> who in turn led United States troops to al-Zarqawi.

Laws are a group's statement of the rules it wants to live by.
These laws may be with the consent of the group, or they may be
imposed by a king or despot. Regardless of their source, although

needed, and sometimes embraced mostly, the laws and those who enforce them are the Common Enemies of the people. We resent those whose job it is to police us and our inner weaknesses.

In his Second Treatise of Civil Government, John Locke (1632-1704), the great English political philosopher wrote:

> For laws not being made for themselves, but to be, by their execution …And he who does it, is justly to be esteemed the common enemy and pest of mankind…

Lawyers, priests, judges, police, teachers, and all others who are the face of the law, and the law itself, are Common Enemies of the willful natures of humans. Those willful natures in each of us make us all vulnerable and sometimes oppositional to the common law. We love the law when it is applied to others, but not so much when it comes after us.

W. H. Auden (1907-1973), the English-born American poet, wrote in "Squares and Oblongs", that:

> Whatever their differences, highbrows and lowbrows have a common enemy, The Law (the Divine as well as the secular),…

Laws and sanctions are the ultimate manipulation of human nature. We create them to manage and organize ourselves and to corral our pagan natures. They are intended, by us, to manipulate and control the Common Enemies we have within us, and to set the rules of relations between us and the outside world. Think treaties and other sets of agreed upon rules.

Now let's look at food. All humans need some amount of it to survive. We all know the appropriate weight ranges for our heights, and many of us know we are overweight, maybe even fat.

Until the age of radio, TV and the Internet, fewer of us were fat. With these new technologies, came advertising geniuses. They sold us on fast food, donuts, pies, late-night eating, sugar, lard and more sugar. And the media, radio and TV made us sedentary as we sat, listened and watched pictures of food scroll across our TV screens.

Obesity and the diseases of cancer, heart disease and diabetes that travel with it, now kill hundreds of thousands of Americans each year. Recognizing this, food education activists are now arguing that Agribusiness and unhealthy foods are dangerous Common Enemies.

McDonald's and other top-notch fast food vendors are rapidly responding. McDonald's changed the oil they cook their French fries in to lower the dangerous trans fats that made their fries taste so great. McDonald's risked upsetting its vaunted fries' superiority to avoid being called a public enemy. That's a worse marketing fate than risking their fries' franchise. Because the current food epidemic kills so many each year, close to the number killed by tobacco, it is foreseeable that food activists will use the Common Enemy threat to educate, manipulate and mobilize the public to declare war on purveyors of sugar and lard. It is also foreseeable that the United States Food and Drug Administration (FDA) will seek Congressional approval to increase the regulation of the content and warnings on foods, as they sought and have now received such unique powers against tobacco from the United States Congress in 2009 when it passed The Family Smoking Prevention and Tobacco Control Act.

Maybe through laws and taxes on unhealthy foods we can respond and control the Common Enemy within each of us that seeks out the sugars and the lards we love to eat. Now, more than ever, gluttony is a Common Enemy and a sin.

Since the United States Surgeon General's report in 1964 on the dangers of tobacco, tobacco has been a Common Enemy, if not Public Enemy #1. Its dangers and costs are so high, society has felt justified in taking hundreds of millions of dollars from the cigarette companies to spread across the United States. This Common Enemy has become a cash cow for governments collecting their sin taxes.

Unfortunately, as Common Enemies go, cigarettes and other tobacco products have been a pernicious Common Enemy. Even today, after all we know and all we've been taught, tobacco products kill approximately 435,000 Americans a year. When deaths from heavy smoking in countries like China, Russia and Eastern Europe are considered, the numbers are staggering.

More costly and painful than these deaths, are the prolonged and costly diseases of lung cancer, cardiovascular events such as heart attacks, strokes, emphysema, and on and on. The healthcare costs of this product exceed 75 billion dollars annually in America.

One of the common questions people ask is how far government should go to fight Common Enemies that are within us, such as substance and food addictions? A libertarian would say that the government should not fight such Common Enemies. It is up to the individual to assume responsibility.

Unfortunately, society bears the costs of individuals who

smoke, eat poorly, ride without motorcycle helmets and engage in other risky behaviors. These costs give society a right to intervene.

If we can't stamp out a Common Enemy so clearly harmful as smoking, we probably can't stamp out similar self-destructive behaviors, like drug use and prostitution. They, too, might be taxed and regulated as cigarettes are. Why waste money futilely fighting Common Enemies that are inherent in human beings and profitable enough to support a Black Market? If there must be such Common Enemies, maybe we should herd and milk them like dairy cows. The income produced could then be used to pay the unavoidable costs of such habits and behaviors.

The last story in this chapter carries two messages. The first shows why people should think before agreeing to city-imposed curfews on their children. The second message shows that when confronted by a Common Enemy, we can act to protect ourselves even if we know we will hurt our neighbors in doing so.

This story starts in St. Louis, Missouri in 2008. St. Louis has a large teenage population, and it has a Metrolink (train). The Metrolink runs by various cities, towns and malls. As more teen-agers congregated, spats and shoplifting got "out of control". A local newspaper headline asked: "Are Teens Becoming the New Common Enemy in St. Louis?"

Such headlines alert and incite teens of a coming war. These teens, by their presence and rowdy acts, spread fear in the older (more powerful) population. First one town on the train route passes a teen curfew and other ordinances that drive the teens on to the next town, and so on. Ultimately, we have a very large number of teens in the last town. Increasingly, they concentrate as they are shut out of more towns. Because of their concentrated numbers, they become a plague, like locusts.

Because these teens have been recognized as Common Enemies, few step forward to assert the right of innocent teens to meet and congregate. Are all teens Common Enemies because some teens break the law? Or, because of the nature of humans, are mobs of teens inherently threatening and dangerous? And is this danger so bad as to justify preventative actions like curfews?

The second message from this story, comes from the question: Can the last town on the train line sue the first town for starting this cascade of teen locusts? The answer is probably "no".

A review of old English law shows that the law excuses wrong-doing if the wrongdoer's defense against a Common Enemy is the cause of injury to an innocent third party. Think of water runoff. We'll get to more on this defense in Chapter 8.

CHAPTER SEVEN

To Scapegoat and To Deflect Attention

An anonymous bard observed that, "A good scapegoat is almost as good as a solution to a problem."

When trying to deflect attention, Common Enemies make good scapegoats. Because no one likes Common Enemies, it doesn't take a big leap of faith to believe that an innocent Common Enemy is the cause of a particular problem.

To deflect attention, it is cheaper and faster to recycle a popular Common Enemy, especially where that Common Enemy has been successfully scapegoated before. Trying to identify and sell a new Common Enemy takes too long and costs too much. Recycle-Reuse.

Take the City Manager who tells taxpayers the city is off-budget because the weather (snow and heat are always good) caused unforeseen costs (snowplowing, salt, overtime charges, air conditioning, etc.). Bad weather has been a Common Enemy since the beginning of time. So almost out of habit, human taxpayers believe the explanation and vote in a new tax. In reality, large executive salaries, benefits and overtime may be the real reasons the city is off-budget.

René Girard (1923-2015), a French-American professor at John Hopkins University, suggests that society solves many of its conflicts by creating scapegoats, such as witches, Jews or outsiders, who are adjudged the cause or source of our problems. The scapegoats are robbed, punished, isolated, expelled and ostracized, creating cohesion and unity against this Common Enemy. The scapegoat becomes a tool of deflection as well as one of unification and manipulation.

A scapegoat, by definition, is innocent, or mostly innocent, of the crime or offense alleged. The scapegoat is blamed for wrongs committed by others, often to hide the real Common Enemy.

Over time, some Common Enemies have become common-coin scapegoats, useful for taking blame for myriad problems.

Because they have been overused, anytime someone says one of these old Common Enemies did some dastardly deed, we should see "red flags". Someone may be trying to deflect us from the true enemy or problem.

A low-cost Common Enemy can save duplicitous leaders a lot of money, while deflecting the scrutiny of their people. While focusing on the Common Enemy, individual groups among the leader's people unite against the Common Enemy. They don't fight among themselves. This saves money, provides unity, internal stability, and it perpetuates the status quo.

If he could talk, Machiavelli's Prince might tell us that every leader, high and low, needs one or more "Common Enemies" to keep the troops' guns pointed in the same direction and away from their leaders.

The greater the wrongs of a leader, the greater the need for a deflection - - a new or recycled Common Enemy will do. The bigger and more dangerous, the better. The Soviet Union needed the Imperial West, and one could argue that Fidel Castro needed the United States to distract his people from the consequences of his failing policies. The United States continues to serve as a Common Enemy for certain South American countries, Cuba, Russia, Iran, North Korea, China and certain African countries.

Through this mechanism the United States helps unify and stabilize this world.

When we convince a foe's people that we will not play the role of their "Common Enemy", the leaders of those people are weakened. The United States should never give our foes the glue and baling wire to hold their shaky regimes together.

Being the global good guy, the white-hatted cowboy, was always a source of American power - - Common Enemy to none and a benefactor to all. Remember the ubiquitous USA Aid burlap bags of rice piled high on the docks of starving countries? Our military might was strongest when shown, but not used. White hat to some, black hat to others. Yin and Yang.

America visibly likes being the good guy, but sometimes it makes blind responses to diminutive Common Enemies. Out of proportion responses, or responses when a non-response is better, tumble America as before Gulliver's Lilliputians. The emotional power of Common Enemies is so great, they can stifle cognition in the brilliant and blind the eyes of visionaries.

Sometimes in our use of Common Enemies, we injure ourselves. As we wear protective gloves and outer garments when we handle nuclear materials, we should be equally cautious when we try to use Common Enemies for our provincial purposes.

Where the Common Enemy is a scapegoat, we must also expect the scapegoat won't like being labeled a Common Enemy. Sometimes these goats have horns and they may butt or gore back.

In 1904, when Russia was on the verge of a revolution, Czar Nicholas II attempted to deflect his population from the need for internal change, starting a small war with Japan. A year later the war ended in Russia's defeat, and 12 years later the Russian Empire fell to revolution. For Russia's deflection to work, it had to prevail over the Common Enemy.

By 1979, Soviet communist rule was fading. The Soviet Union invaded Afghanistan but failed to prevail. Twelve years later the Soviet Union disintegrated. Common Enemies can only do so much work and the deflection effort is likely to fail when the Common Enemy is not defeated.

Finally, we again look at Adolf Hitler. He learned how to use scapegoats and Common Enemies to deflect and manipulate a populace from the great German leader, Otto von Bismarck, the man who brought us WWI.

Hitler and his party could do nothing of substance to address the economic ruin that was Germany after WWI. Hitler needed to blame someone for Germany's ills so Germans wouldn't blame him and his emerging party as he rose to power on the backs of his scapegoats. He needed Common Enemies to motivate and unify a down-and-out Germany. He needed someone to blame. Von Bismarck used Catholic Common Enemy scapegoats to unify Germans before WWI; Hitler used the Jews. Germany's economic ruin was caused by money-manipulating banker Jews, Hitler told his people. And many of his people were pre-primed to accept this explanation as it played into a German history of anti-Semitism.

Hitler used the Jews first as scapegoats, and then, because of the alleged wrongs they committed against the German people, these otherwise innocent scapegoats became existential Enemies of the State.

As Common Enemies of the German state, Jews were denigrated, dehumanized, despised and exterminated.

Because Jews were a despised Common Enemy, the holocaust became possible. Everyone saw it happening and few wanted to believe it or get involved. Few had the courage to stand in front of a fast-moving bandwagon. A mob was on the move. It became the zeitgeist. No one in or out of Germany acted to stop Hitler and his madness.

CHAPTER EIGHT

To Excuse or Justify Action or Inaction

The threat posed by a Common Enemy such as water, may be so great as to justify and excuse adverse consequences caused by a landowner's precipitous actions taken in defense against that Common Enemy.

Hundreds of years ago, the English courts adopted the Common Enemy doctrine. This rule recognizes that because surface water is a Common Enemy to all landowners, landowners have the right to alter the drainage pattern of their lands (ponds, ditches, dikes and the like) without regard to how this might affect a neighbor's land. This doctrine continues today in most American states, in some form, as the Common Enemy Doctrine.

Because we all inherently recognize the threat Common Enemies pose to our survival, we are more willing to excuse breaches in the social contract as certain otherwise unacceptable actions are taken in order to protect us from our Common Enemies, even if our neighbor's land and house get flooded. Our survival against the threat of a Common Enemy comes first. From an evolutionary perspective survival is the first imperative.

High and important values will be abandoned by civilized people gripped by the fear of a Common Enemy. After the Japanese attack on Pearl Harbor on December 7, 1941, Japan and the Japanese became America's Common Enemy. Setting aside its own United States Constitution, America imprisoned thousands of American citizens of Japanese descent. Not because they did anything wrong, but because they were Japanese and they might do something wrong. Americans were afraid of Japanese-American saboteurs. Common Enemies excused America's actions against its own citizens, and the presence of Common Enemies excused behavior that was a patent violation of core American values.

Although America was concurrently at war with Germany, German-Americans weren't imprisoned or interned. Americans of German descent looked like the white male power structure of the time. They were bonded with us by their common features, values and looks. Because the Japanese looked different, common bonding was absent, and the Japanese got interned. Is racism another word for this?

America excused itself from following its rules because it was confronted by a Common Enemy.

Having looked at how Common Enemies are used as excuses for precipitous actions, let's now look at how Common Enemies are used as excuses for inaction and failure.

During WWII in early 1942, Franklin D. Roosevelt sent a "sorry" letter to His Highness Sidi Moncef Pacha Bey of Tunis, paraphrased: I can't help you in Tunis because I am fighting Common Enemies [elsewhere]. In other words, I'm sorry I can't help you, but I am fighting our Common Enemies somewhere else.

By November 9, 1942, Roosevelt needed something. He wrote again to the Pacha Bey, this time promising that:

> The indomitable and massive American armed forces which I am dispatching to North Africa, in collaboration with the force of France, will cooperate with you in the defense of your country. They have no other aim than the early *destruction of our common enemies*. They and their allies hope for the great

privilege of passage through Tunisia thus enabling them to accomplish their mission-the elimination of the forces of evil from North Africa. (Italics added)

President Roosevelt needed a military staging area for the Allied North African Campaign against the Nazis.

Now let's look at Cuba. Common Enemies sprouted there and on America's South Florida shores in the early 1950s.

The mountain jungle rebel Fidel Castro overthrows Cuban President Batista, a corrupt American puppet. Becoming a Communist, Castro dispossesses the landed and privileged Cuban classes who flee 90 miles to South Florida in the United States. Their Cuban lands are redistributed to "the people". These two parts of a common people became Common Enemies to each other. Besides, a Communist Cuba was also a Soviet surrogate. This way, America could have low-intensity conflict with the Soviets, and the dispossessed Cubans in America could continue hostilities with Cuba's current government.

The United States saw Castro and his Communist government as a Common Enemy, a direct threat to America's way of life and its regard for private property. The Soviets provided Castro with support and in exchange, the right to place defensive Inter-Continental Ballistic Missiles (ICBMs) in Cuba, only 90 miles from the United States. Years later Americans learned the Soviets did this apparent Cuban provocation because the United States had earlier placed American ICBM's in Turkey, 90 miles from the Soviet border.

From all of this, the Americans and Soviets had the

Cuban Missile Crisis. Publicly, the Soviets backed down and removed their missiles from Cuba. Secretly, America removed its missiles from Turkey. John F. Kennedy, the young Prince, enhanced himself by vanquishing a Common Enemy, or at least that is how the story was told in America and the Western Press for years.

The Soviet Union has crumbled, yet today, decades later, Cuba remains America's Common Enemy. Cuba is isolated, embargoed and strangled in all possible ways. Like the Palestinians in Israel and neighboring refugee camps, many of the Cuban elite that fled to America hope they will one day be able to return to their land and recover their homes and property. This unrealistic hope pressures the U.S. to continue its sanctions on Cuba.

Meanwhile, in spite of being the target of America's might, decades later, successors of the Castro regime continue to rule. They continue in spite of great poverty and the suppression of basic civil liberties. Ironically, the regime bonds its people in unity by using an all too willing America, as their great Common Enemy. One could argue that the Castro regime continues because of America and not in spite of it.

One has to wonder how many decades the Castro-type regime will survive because America plays the obliging role of Common Enemy. America's sanctions help the regime argue that Cuba's travails are caused by United States and not the regime's failed collective policies.

In 2023, it became apparent that India's Prime Minister, Narendra Modi, was allowing, if not encouraging, pogroms against Muslims and Christians. Whether his motivation was the achievement of a pure Hindu nationalistic state or was the result of his attempt to appease Hindu voters, his failure to prevent pogroms is abhorrent to American values and interests, yet America failed to take action. This inaction can be explained by America's greater interest in maintaining its friendship with India because India, the most populous nation in the world, has seen its neighbor China as a Common Enemy for decades. Thus, abhorrent Indian religious nationalism was allowed to pass because ... "The enemy of my enemy (China) is my friend."

Common Enemies, real or imagined, have clout. They drive us to action, distraction and inaction. The fear of them gives us license to engage in thoughtless action and thoughtful inaction. Our actions against Common Enemies are also used to excuse both base and inhuman actions that break most of our social contracts. Yet we continue our fated dance with Common Enemies because they also often serve our purposes.

Ultimately, when evil or reckless people abuse Common Enemies, horrible and ugly behaviors can emerge. And the escalation of these behaviors may lead to unforeseen consequences. Because the power of Common Enemies is great, the potential for danger and harm is also great.

Once the label of Common Enemy is placed on a target group or individual, denigration, confiscation and extermination (genocide) of the target group can result. When hate and dehumanization reach a boiling point, the Common Enemy target group is primed for extermination. Such are the passions and power Common Enemies can generate.

CHAPTER NINE

To Denigrate, Confiscate and Exterminate

Once labeled a Common Enemy, any person, group or state so labeled is at risk of death. Getting labeled a Common Enemy is like getting a Black Spot from a Robert Louis Stevenson pirate. It's bad news. If only in the defense of one's position, the defensive battle itself will be costly. Where lives are at risk, these are the highest of stakes. Can you imagine being labeled a Common Enemy, or Public Enemy No. 1 and having America's Federal Bureau of Investigation (FBI) coming after you?

After the December 21, 1988 bombing of Pan Am 103 over Lockerbie, Scotland by Libyan agents, Libya's dictator Muammar Gaddafi was labeled Common Enemy No. 1 by the world. In the decades since, under global pressure, this Common Enemy dropped his dream of acquiring weapons of mass destruction. For a time this volatile and reckless man was accepted as a reformed citizen by most of the world. His multi-million dollar payout and an admission of responsibility for the bombing, was our rich Common Enemy's response to global pressure. Gaddafi seemed to recognize he could live longer and do better business if he was not labeled a Common Enemy.

That was the plan. But Common Enemy Gaddafi could not change his stripes. In 2009, after Scotland released the Pan Am bomber mastermind because he was dying of cancer, Gaddafi held a high-profile Welcome Home to Libya party for this mass murderer. With this act, and a hateful world speech delivered to the United Nations Assembly in the fall of 2009, General Gaddafi returned himself to the pantheon of Common Enemies, or just possibly, the pantheon of world-class wackos. In 2011,

General Gaddafi was killed by National Transition Council forces in support of a NATO mission in Libya

Is it possible any of us could become a Common Enemy by killing a young family while driving drunk? It could happen that easily.

On the other side of the coin, we are more likely to become part of a group that labels another group a Common Enemy than be labeled a Common Enemy ourselves. Barring criminal acts, we are unlikely to be labeled a Common Enemy ourselves

Before a group forms, something happens. Someone in the society will see a Common Enemy and alert the citizens to the real or perceived Common Enemy. Victims, touters, hawkers and other leaders will unite the group by beating the drum, warning of the danger posed by the Common Enemy. Evolutionary survival probably tunes our ears to hear these warning drumbeats.

Rallying the citizens by fingering a Common Enemy is a precondition to war. Some rallying cries will be answered, and some will not. The following example shows how American President Teddy Roosevelt used a Common Enemy to institute the United States personal income tax that Americans know so well today.

Before income taxes became a permanent fixture in America, Teddy Roosevelt, a progressive icon, recognized the great disparity of wealth across America, and he recognized that the government needed more money to do the great projects he envisioned. He wanted to redistribute income and he wanted the average American to get a "Square Deal".

Setting the stage for the first permanent federal taxation of private wealth, he declared that the rich were "...malefactors of great wealth". Malefactors being defined as people who break the law and do evil.

The rich were declared outlaws, and they became a class of Common Enemies of the people. The rich controlled trusts, banks and most of America's wealth. The common American was incensed by the greed and opulent lifestyle of this class. Against this anger, a wave of public support for taxation rose. The wealthy, portrayed as gluttons, saw their world drastically change.

Teddy made the rich *bad*. He denigrated the corpulent, selfish class. Indeed, it was class warfare. Greed and gluttony, after all, are among the seven deadly sins. Since 1913, this income tax, a blessing and a curse, has been an American fixture.

Nineteen years later, in July of 1932, Teddy Roosevelt's cousin Franklin was President of the United States as an ongoing economic world depression crushed the lives of American citizens. Like his cousin before him, Franklin declared that Common Enemies were: the depression; the republican policies that brought the depression; hunger; and being dispossessed. To combat these Common Enemies Franklin Delano Roosevelt proposed a New Deal for the American people. Schemes for the building of infrastructure, the employment of the unemployed, even including writers, actors and artists, redistributed great amounts of wealth to the lower levels of the societal pyramid, and in the process, stimulated the economy and its recovery.

People who are fed, people who are working and people

who have places to live were unlikely to pursue revolution, communism and other forms of social disorder. Although the opposition called Franklin Roosevelt a socialist, he may have saved capitalism and democracy in America as well as feeding millions of hungry mouths by recognizing the dignity of millions of now-working Americans.

Few want to give comfort to or associate with a *bad* or denigrated Common Enemy. This results in the group's isolation of the Common Enemy.

Once isolated, the target-victim group is per se, outside of society. Those outside our society are somehow less human. They are not us. They are disenfranchised, and we soon develop a language to dehumanize them. They are at risk of physical danger at this point. The target victims mean little to us, and only our training, motivation, experiences and values offer any solace or benefit of the doubt to such Common Enemies.

Sometimes when confronted by the danger of a Common Enemy, if the danger is sufficiently prolonged, fear, revulsion and hate festers. And if the danger persists at an intolerable level, the weaker and previously submissive victim may fight back even if it means certain death, if only to end its own pain. In one famous example, the Jewish rebels on Masada committed mass suicide in 73 CE rather than give the Romans the pleasure of victory.

To label a person or group a Common Enemy, is to declare that designee an outlaw without rights. To the Romans, the rebel Israelites were a Common Enemy threat to Roman power. This ensured that the Romans, in turn, were the Common Enemy of the Jews on Masada.

From antiquity until the international treaties of the mid-1900s (after which conquerors could not, under international law, legally keep conquered land), it was conflict tradition that, in defeat, conquered Common Enemies lost their land, their liberty and their lives. The theory behind this current proscription is that future wars will be less likely if land acquisition through war is proscribed.

Once the American Indian was declared a Common Enemy by the colonial English, their lands were taken, and the Indians themselves were relocated, sold as slaves or killed. In this case, who was the Common Enemy, the colonists, the natives or both? History now, albeit too late, considers the colonists the precipitating-invading Common Enemy, another case where the wrong-doing aggressor benefits from the wrong, and the wrongdoers get the land.

Captured Common Enemies, whether innocent or guilty, are given little quarter.

In 1788, the Constitutional Convention of Virginia declared that:

>...A pirate, an outlaw, or a common enemy to
>all mankind, may be put to death at any time.
>It is justified by the laws of nature and nations.

There is no mention of Due Process of Law. Common Enemies are bugs to be stamped out. Or so the thinking goes.

Today, Common Enemies of the people of the United States of America (pirates, organized criminals, drug dealers, etc.) all face forfeiture laws and imprisonment, if not death. It is presumed that all of the property and possessions these Common Enemies have, are ill-gotten gains, subject to forfeiture.

Few of us want to do bad things to innocent people. But most of us are willing to do very bad things to bad people or people we believe are bad. Bad groups such as the Hell's Angels, the Crips and other street gangs, are indicted as a group in the public's eye. Innocent individuals in the group are guilty because their tribe is a Common Enemy.

Such human and group responses to Common Enemies are motivated by the evolutionary imperative of survival. Few of these Common Enemies should expect any quarter.

Once formed to do battle against a Common Enemy, the victim group may misread the motivation of its aggressor. Maybe the aggressor is not out to avenge a wrong, maybe the aggressor is simply using Common Enemy declarations to justify the theft (confiscation) of property, of land and of life. Indeed, this is often the case. Conquest for booty, sounds better if marketed as a battle against a Common Enemy.

Where land and loot is the aggressor's goal, and where the aggressor has a surplus of people, the target group, if declared a Common Enemy, can expect genocide if they are defeated. Dead people don't return to get back their property and land. The aggressor's attack is justified in the public relations of the world because the vanquished was, after all, a Common Enemy.

As Adolf Hitler rose to power, he played Common Enemy cards like Itzhak Perlman plays a violin. He was ironically done in because he finally made and united too many Common Enemies.

Adolf Hitler was born in Austria on April 20, 1889. He was rejected from art school because he couldn't or wouldn't paint human figures. His architectural and landscape paintings were tight and competent. He joined the Nazi party in 1919, and was jailed in 1923 after a failed coup in Bavaria. He gained power by touting German nationalism, anti-Semitism and anti-communism. While he led Germany between 1933 and 1945, millions of Jews, Gypsies, homosexuals and other Common Enemies of his Third Reich were systematically exterminated in one of the largest genocides in human history. Hitler committed suicide in 1945. Photograph courtesy of FreeImages.

An overview of Hitler's use, abuse and finally justice at the hands of his Common Enemies illustrates many of the points intended for this chapter. As he rose to power, Hitler instigated conflicts with targeted enemies to advance his career. He looked for cleavages to exploit. Early on, he pitted rural folk against city dwellers. Jews dwelled in the city. Jews had been someone's Common Enemies for thousands of years. Hitler declared that Jews were Common Enemies to Aryan racial purity. Jews, homosexuals and others threatened the survival of all Aryans. Each was linked with the other. Hitler denigrated and abused them. He built much of this on antipathy and a backdrop of historic anti-Semitism.

Hitler's henchmen burned down the German Reichstag and then blamed the dirty deed on his political opposition. He labeled them Common Enemies of the state. He staged a coup. His political opposition, now weakened by the Reichstag scandal, was vanquished, and he became the leader of the German state.

Gypsies, the retarded and other less than prime Aryan specimens were shipped to concentration camps. Jews rode the same trains.

Hitler's extermination of six million Jews in less than five years ranks this genocide as one of the largest in the history of mankind. But because the German people viewed Jews and others as subhuman Common Enemies, their loss was neither understood nor grieved until after the war, and the German mob came back to its objective senses.

Early in the war, Hitler wisely signed a non-aggression pact with Stalin and the Soviets. This meant Hitler did not have to devote men and material to defend, or attack, an Eastern Front. Some say Hitler would have won the war if he had honored that pact.

Instead, Hitler attacked the Soviets and became their Common Enemy, and the Soviets became a Common Enemy to Hitler. At this point it was only a matter of time before Hitler lost the war. With Britain, the Soviets, and then the United States against him, he had one too many Common Enemies on too many fronts.

Currently, the United States has Donald J. Trump, a master in the use of Common Enemies, second only to Hitler. Like Hitler, Mr. Trump used Common Enemies to advance his political career.

Before running for president, he declared that five young black men suspected in a Central Park rape of a white jogger were "GUILTY" in a full-page ad in the New York Times. This ad got him national attention and helped establish him as a "tough on crime" politician. When these five young men were later proved to be innocent, Mr. Trump never retracted or apologized for his defamatory ad.

To help himself get elected to the U.S. presidency he declared that Muslims were terrorists. He also slandered immigrants by claiming they were all criminals, drug smugglers and disease-carrying. To fight these Common Enemies he created a slogan, "Build the Wall", to protect Americans from this invading hoard coming from south of the border. When members of the press criticized some of his slanders, he declared the Media a Common Enemy. Next, when U.S. civil servants in the course of their jobs resisted some of Mr. Trump's questionable programs or policies, he declared them Deep State Enemies. He denigrated the

Media, and he made popular "alternative facts" as he disregarded actual facts.

When certain agencies of the federal government started to investigate Mr. Trump's nefarious activities, he labeled the Federal Bureau of Investigation (FBI) a Common Enemy. And when FBI investigations led to prosecutions by the U.S. Department of Justice, Mr. Trump declared these prosecutions part of a politically motivated deep state conspiracy against him. And when these investigations lead to criminal prosecutions, Mr. Trump and his Republican allies accused President Biden, the successor president, of "weaponizing" the Department of Justice. As the prosecutions multiplied in state and federal courts it became apparent that he, like Hitler, may have too many Common Enemies on too many fronts.

Like Hitler, Donald Trump is an arch propagandist of our time. He uses Common Enemies as a strategy to mold the opinions and attitudes of Americans for his own purposes. Division, chaos, doubt and fear are the weapons he uses against any person or institution that challenges him and against any individuals or institutions that try to hold him accountable. During the divorce from his first wife Ivana, she testified that Trump's favorite book, the book he kept by his bedside, was a compilation of Hitler's speeches titled "My New Order". As to Hitler's tactics and techniques, Mr. Trump was an excellent student. Photograph courtesy of Fulton County, Georgia.

Not all this denigration, theft and injury by and to Common Enemies involves nations and world leaders. It also happens to a lesser degree in American high schools across the country.

One group of kids for a real, feigned or no reason at all, labels another group, "weirdos, goths, jocks, nerds", etc. in order to denigrate and lessen them. It is also done to advance the social status of the aggressors. These are acts of bullying. Power and evolutionary struggle is at work even in school.

Lies, slanders and other charges can turn the targets of these slurs into a Common Enemy. Those so labeled may be shunned, mobbed, robbed and hurt. Blacks have been lynched in the American South, and gays have been bled to death after being strung up on a barbed wire fence because they were someone's Common Enemy.

Every genocide is done for a reason. And each reason usually relates to the survival of the group from the threat of a Common Enemy or an excuse to seize land and property.

In the mid-1990s, Rwanda's Hutu majority tribe decided that the immigrant Tutsis were outsiders, encroaching on their land. But this was nothing new. The Tutsis had been doing so for four hundred years. The Hutu radio station, Radio Télévision Libre des Milles (RTLM) beat the drums of hate, racism and impending extermination. When the RTLM referred to Tutsis as cockroaches that must be exterminated, the Tutsis were ripe for genocide. The Hutus wanted the Tutsis' land and property. And they wanted the Tutsis gone forever.

This pile of Tutsi skulls is the end point of Hutu genocide against the Tutsis, who suffered up to 800,000 deaths in 100 days.

Between 1975 and 1979, Cambodia's Khmer Rouge leader, Pol Pot, killed 2 million Cambodians as he tried to create an agrarian society by killing members of the "Old Society". The wealthy, doctors, lawyers, former government officials and police, and their families, were labeled Common Enemies of the people. "What is rotten must be removed", was a Khmer Rouge mantra. Pol Pot focused his killing on the Vietnamese, Chinese and Cham Muslim minorities. In April, 1998, 73 year-old Pol Pot died of a heart attack before he could be brought to trial.

Genocide, extermination and death are the extreme risks faced by people or groups labeled Common Enemies. On December 9, 1948, the United Nations ratified the first international convention against genocide. Photograph courtesy of UCLA.

During the genocide that followed, RTLM urged listeners to "exterminate the Tutsi from the globe." "Make them disappear once and for all."

At the beginning of the Hutu build-up to genocide, Hutu leaders told their race, "Tutsi are nomads and invaders who came to Rwanda in search of pasture." If they take my land, they take my life. Those who would take my life are my Common Enemies.

Because the Hutu people bought this Common Enemy ruse and because believing this benefitted them, they became killer mercenaries in a horrible modern genocide.

We would like to hope that in the rational light of day, many Hutus now see that they, as individuals in a group, did great wrongs while drunk on the power that comes from within when a mob battles a Common Enemy.

Common Enemies stimulate fear. Fear stimulates responses. But hopefully we respond softly when the slight is small. And when the injury is great and unprovoked, hopefully time allows us to make a thoughtful and proportional response. Unless of course the agenda from the onset is theft from and death to a Common Enemy. Such motivations must be recognized early and combatted with vigor.

Because Common Enemies are also always within us (such as the seven deadly sins), we should try to understand why we do what we do. We should also recognize that internal conflicts can cause us to view ourselves as a Common Enemy. Self-loathing, self-destructive behavior and suicide are rungs on that ladder. Hate is a response that can lead to genocide and the deaths of ourselves and others.

When external Common Enemies appear, when we can, we should take time to think and consider a proportional response, or no response at all if the Common Enemy is too large and dangerous, or too small or remote a threat. Sometimes responding to a gnat creates a bigger problem than no response at all, although one has been bitten. Would we use a hammer to kill a bug that lands on our nose? On the other hand, if the Common Enemy is too large and too dangerous for us to reasonably fight, no response is probably our best initial response.

External Common Enemies are often not the danger they first appear to be. Where possible, understand the motives of the aggressor or the roots of the problem. Be slow to declare an aggressor or a problem a Common Enemy because that locks the parties into a heightened conflict, and the clarion caller doesn't want to lose credibility by "crying wolf".

Some external Common Enemies, especially deadly diseases and bodies heading toward earth from space, need to be eradicated. We don't have to think too long, nor do we need to understand the motives of dread diseases or impending asteroid strikes.

But where people and groups are involved as Common Enemies, or possible Common Enemies, caution and thought are good behaviors.

War, extermination and genocide are the end points of resolving disputes with human Common Enemies. If one looks at the continuum of response options available when confronted by a Common Enemy, genocide is at the extreme end of the continuum. As a word, genocide was not used until Raphael Lemkin first used the term to describe the Nazi atrocities during the Nuremberg trials after WWII.

Before this, terms such as ethnic cleansing, war and atrocities were used.

Professor Mark Lund hypothesized that a critical amount of intelligence is required for genocide. He is probably right. But until 1978 when Jane Goodall made startling observations in chimpanzees, most of us believed only humans were intelligent enough and technically capable of committing genocide. In 1986, Dr. Goodall reported that one tribe of chimpanzees exterminated another tribe of chimpanzees living on the other side of the same island despite the fact that they had previously lived together. This chimpanzee slaughter is frightening. It shows how base human genocide is. In spite of this example of animal mayhem, genocide is an act seen almost exclusively in humans. Or better stated, genocide is committed by intelligent humans who have also evolved sophisticated killing technologies.

It takes a group and tools to kill an entire people. One killer cannot kill an entire people. At least not yet, as no such individual weapon has yet been invented.

Genocide has received extensive academic scrutiny since WWII and the Nazi holocaust against the Jews. After the war, captured records confirmed what many had suspected. The holocaust was planned by the Nazis as a final solution: the genocide of the Jewish people. It was no accident or practice that slowly evolved. It was an engineered plan.

Researchers have found that genocide usually benefits the aggressor-perpetrator. Researchers have studied the motivations of genocide. They find that scarcity of resources (territory, food or sex) is the most common motivation for genocide.

Other historic motivations, including racial purity, religion and revenge (payback) are also stimulated by primal survival mechanisms.

How then does one motivate a group to act in concert to mobilize to kill all members of another group? Appealing to primal fears and dehumanizing Common Enemies are the behaviors that set the scene for genocidal acts.

The following historic timeline of human genocide reveals the common stimulants of genocide and ethnic cleansing.

In 1948 genocide was defined for the first time by the U.N. Convention on the Prevention and Punishment of the Crime of Genocide (Article 2):

> ...acts committed with intent to destroy, in whole or in part, a national, ethnical, racial or religious group, as such: killing members of the group; causing serious bodily or mental harm to members of the group; deliberately inflicting on the group conditions of life, calculated to bring about its physical destruction in whole or in part; imposing measures intended to prevent births within the group; [and] forcibly transferring children of the group to another group.

The destruction of Common Enemies may be as old as

organized society. Groups could not kill other groups until the first groups formed. Genocide appeared simultaneously or soon after the first groups formed.

Around 30,000 BCE, French paleoanthropologist Marcillin Boule hypothesized in 1912, Homo sapiens exterminated Neanderthals. Wow. Think of the implications, possibly the first human genocide. The first ethnic cleansing may have occurred 32,000 years ago and, if true, this act may be the result of hardwiring that has predestined our family tree. Unfortunately, we will probably never know the truth of this question, but it would explain the Neanderthals' apparent disappearance or absorption.

The first *written* history of genocide appears in the Old Testament of the Bible. God told Moses (and the Israelites) to kill all the Midian men, boys and post-pubescent women. Virginal girls were to be saved and bred into the tribes of Israel. The Midians were viewed as Common Enemies, and God told the Israelites (Deuteronomy 9:1-6) "...you are going to take possession of their lands...on account of the wickedness of these nations." Unless God really told Moses to kill the Midians, this genocide was simply a land grab.

In 146 BCE, Rome's genocide of Carthage ended the Third Punic War. It ended a century of conflict between Rome and Carthage over colonial expansion. Roman fear, hatred and desire for revenge against Carthage for Hannibal's attacks on Rome in the Second Punic War probably motivated this genocide. Too much fear over too many years made genocide seem rational. Rome never wanted to war with Carthage again. Thus, Carthage was totally sacked.

Between 1500 and 1900 CE, over ten million Native Americans were exterminated according to University of Hawaii history professor David Stannard. In his opinion, Native Americans suffered the "...worst human holocaust the world had ever witnessed..." taking over ten million lives over four centuries. Native Americans were killed by the intentional distribution of smallpox-infected blankets, scalp bounties, enslavement, starvation and re-location." They had land. The new Americans wanted it and they took it. Again the aggressor Common Enemy benefitted, in part, by successfully labeling the victim a savage and heathen Common Enemy.

In 1915, the Ottoman Turkish Government used WWI as cover for the genocide of the Armenian people. The Turks killed and systematically removed the Armenians from a homeland they had occupied for 3000 years. Again, land acquisition was the Turk's goal.

Beginning in 1940, the Nazis began a genocide of Jews, Gypsies, the handicapped, homosexuals, Jehovah's Witnesses, social democrats and anyone else seen as an obstacle to Hitler's dream of racial purity and lebensraum.

Between 1956 and 2001, there was genocide against Tamils by the Sinhala Buddhist Government in Sri Lanka. Sri Lankans wanted the Tamils' land.

Between 1975 and 1979, the Khmer Rouge rulers of Cambodia killed 25% of Cambodia's population: the "old society" of the educated, the wealthy, Buddhist monks, police, doctors, lawyers, teachers and former government officials. The Common Enemies of the new peasant people's government were exterminated. The old power elite was gone, and because of genocide, it would never return to reclaim its property or its place.

Finally, in 1986, renowned primatologist Jane Goodall reported the first known case of non-human genocide. After years of co-existence on an island, when confronted by diminishing resources, the tribe of chimpanzees from one side of the island went to the other side of the island to kill all members of the second tribe in what was called the Four-Year War. This shocking genocide has given evidence to what some researchers had hypothesized, that genocide and ethnic cleansing have evolutionary and biological bases. For those who believe in Darwin's theory, real or imagined survival, especially in the face of limited resources, may be a driver of genocide.

By definition, competing groups are each other's Common Enemies. And when the duration and intensity of the competition reaches a tipping point, genocide becomes an emotional and seemingly rational choice. On the other hand, one must always be aware that so-called Common Enemies may be innocent scapegoats targeted for their possessions, their land and various other reasons, including revenge. But are we concerned about being just? If history is a guide, we more likely want land and property.

In 1994, Rwanda's Hutus began exterminating the Tutsi minority. The Hutu majority wanted to ethnically cleanse the minority Tutsis who were viewed as territorial encroachers. The

Tutsi were also viewed as being part of the Belgium colonial power base of the past that had committed offenses against the Hutus for many years. Payback can be a bitch.

From this genocide timeline (32,000 BCE – today CE), we can see that genocide is nothing new, and we can see that genocide is still with us today.

It's still a jungle out there.

SECTION III
CHAPTER TEN

Considerations

Common Enemies have always been within us and around us.

There will always be Common Enemies. Some will be real, and some will be bogus: set-ups and scapegoats being used as tools by skillful and sometimes corrupt actors.

The power of Common Enemies to boil our blood and rocket us to group action probably has no equal. Common Enemies pierce our primordial souls. Our evolutionary growth, as we struggle for survival as a species, is driven more by Common Enemies than any other factors, excepting food and sex. Ironically, sometimes we can secure food and sex by declaring a target group a Common Enemy to justify the taking of their food and women.

An information highway carries warnings about looming Common Enemies, real or fake. Originally this information highway was word of mouth; then horseback; then telegraph; telephone; radio and television. Each technology faster than the one before. Now we have tweets (X) and texts, faster still.

There are benefits and costs associated with the increase in speed these technologies bring. One benefit is the ability to warn and educate lots of people in a hurry. A cost could be the rapid spread of a big lie. The speed of today's technology is a major factor in enhancing the power of Common Enemy tools for good and evil.

In evolutionary theory, mutations either succeed or fail depending on their ability to survive against their Common Enemies in nature. That which doesn't kill us makes us stronger. And adaptations that keep us from being killed are evolutionary successes.

The oriental concepts of Yin and Yang suggest that there are complementary opposites within each environment. These opposites constantly interact and never reach equilibrium. They are opposites bound together. For example, a species with only males and no females would quickly die out. Interaction between the two creates babies and continues the species.

Yin and Yang are the balanced opposites of hard and soft, sweet and sour, strong and weak, wet and dry, white and black, good and evil, rich and poor, life and death, and so on.

If all of this is so, then war, whether hot or cold, is the common fate of our species. War is perpetual because humans have a biological-evolutionary imperative that seems to require it. When we don't have a Common Enemy, we seek one out or create one. Common Enemies are the caffeine in our morning coffee.

Common Enemies prepare us and our psyches for war and conflict. Historically, against our Common Enemies, we have fought to protect that which is ours and sometimes to seize that which is theirs. It is often reflex that brings us to war over assets, property, land, oil or a scummy water-well in an expansive desert, as we have fought over such things since the beginning of time. It is the Common Enemy that threatens whatever we hold dear. Yet, we are often the dreaded villain that is the Common Enemy to our Common Enemy. Yin and Yang.

As irritating as Common Enemies are to us, we create new ones for our own purposes if old Common Enemies are not handy.

On the theory that humanity is always in motion and abhors stasis, it is foreseeable that in the absence of literal, in your face

Common Enemies, humans will create and denigrate Common Enemies for one or more of the many uses previously described. If there are no lions, tigers and bears on the prowl, we seek conceptual Common Enemies like the devil and sin. Each, always around and within us. Humans seem to need the fear and adrenaline Common Enemies bring, as humans need oxygen to breathe.

Sometimes, truly dangerous Common Enemies approach us, but we are slow to see and respond to them because we do not recognize the danger.

Late in the 20th century, for example, world scientists warned of impending environmental doom due to Global Warming caused by the release of carbon dioxide and other gases into the atmosphere. Predictions, speeches and even a movie by former United States Vice President Al Gore warned of the dangers to come.

These early warnings were heeded by few. Our species had too much invested in a high CO_2 emissions lifestyle: cars, planes, cement and incandescent light bulbs. As time passes, and dire predictions start to come true (e.g., the melting of the polar ice caps), more of us will pay more attention.

High mileage automobile engines, smoke-stack scrubbers and other adaptations began to appear. It makes sense that the more imminent and real the danger, the faster and stronger a group's response to the Common Enemy. Unfortunately, with Common Enemies like global warming, the consequences come on slowly over an extended period of time. Such Common

Enemies are often hard to rally against because our society takes a long time to sense fear when the threat is new, is contested and is not blatant or imminent.

It is probably true that the greater the threat perceived, the greater the chance of a prompt and adequate response.

Because of human variances due to training, intelligence and experience, it is difficult to say whether Newton's Third Law of Motion applies, that is, for every action there is an equal and opposite reaction.

Because of variances in our species, it is probable that Newton's Third Law does not apply. Some humans are slow to provoke, and others have a short fuse. Some are crafty and others are dull. Some use a sledge hammer on every problem, and others are reluctant to strike back at all. And even though Psalm 37:11 predicts that the meek shall inherit the earth, nature tends to prove the opposite. Natives, such as the Indians in North America or the Aborigines in Australia, were usually too slow and too technologically challenged to fight back effectively. All too often they are pushed off their land or exterminated. Darwin v. Psalm 37:11.

In our daily lives, our species fights the Common Enemies of hunger and disease. Even today, great swaths of Africa suffer starvation on an epic scale, while diseases still wrack the poor around the world. These Common Enemies will always be with us. And we will always fight these Common Enemies to ensure our survival as a species. We may even win or hold the line in some of these battles. After all, until the 1900s, few people lived into their 60s and 70s. Today, people living into their 90s and 100s are increasingly common.

Today, hunger and disease are literal Common Enemies that still exist. We can see malnourished children in magazine ads appealing for funds. Today we can see diseases under a microscope. We can understand them, even if we cannot yet treat all of them. These understandings which reduce fear have come from accumulated knowledge and from technological advances, some as simple as a microscope.

As recently as 150 years ago, most disease was mysterious. Faith healers, witch doctors and shamans ruled. No one yet understood germ theory. Until Louis Pasteur's discovery of germs in 1861, it was angry gods or witches casting spells that caused disease and death. People labeled "witches" were hung or burned at the stake because we knew of no better way to fight the Common Enemies of disease and death.

The less understood a Common Enemy is, the greater the chance our responses to these Common Enemies will be wrong. Burning witches never prevented a plague.

The less understood a Common Enemy is, the greater mischief a bad or evil leader can achieve by rallying the group against that Common Enemy. Common Enemies we don't understand tend to provoke more fear than Common Enemies we know and can cognitively access. Solar eclipses, for example, caused great fear in early humans. Without the sun, humans were doomed. Today, we know that solar eclipses are temporary, routine and safe astrological events.

Nebulous "Common Enemies" are insidiously dangerous

because they are difficult to expose, define and rebut. It is hard to push a cloud. This gives the promoter of nebulous Common Enemies an advantage over the contemplative skeptic.

The more nebulous the Common Enemy, the more power the manipulator of the Common Enemy has (such as George W. Bush's "War on Terror": What is Terror? Al-Qaeda? Taliban? Iraq & Saddam Hussein? Chechens? IRA? FARC? Aryan Nations? Arab Americans?). After President Bush's War on Terror declaration, he could do whatever he wanted to do without Congressional approval by steamrolling the population into hatred, action and war against the amorphous Common Enemy, terrorism. By declaring X, Y or Z a terrorist, a supporter of terrorism, a terrorist enterprise, President Bush took license to do as he pleased.

It may be best to respond slowly and with caution when a crier promotes a new ill-defined or nebulous Common Enemy.

To avoid the danger of being bulldozed into taking a wrong action, we should respond slowly and cognitively to nebulous or newly emerging Common Enemies. Ask: Who is promoting this new Common Enemy? What are the motivations of this promoter? Does this "Common Enemy" pose a real danger to our tribe? Is this "Common Enemy" a threat to me? Is that threat imminent or theoretical?

The more triggers pulled (emotions provoked) by a Common Enemy, the more powerful that Common Enemy is, for good or for bad.

As Common Enemies and their targets or mutual Common

Enemies interact, each interaction heightens the power and intensity of the conflict. Finally, one of two things happens, settlement or combat.

When leaders use Common Enemies to unite or distract their people, they should choose Common Enemies that provoke great fear and are poorly understood. When time is short, they should use Common Enemies that their people have historically recognized as fearsome and deserving of destruction. It's easier to sell an old and long-held fear when you don't have to start from scratch by finding and selling a new Common Enemy.

Anytime you see the "Common Enemy" button pushed by anyone, see red flags. Except for confirmed incoming nuclear missiles, most "imminent" dangers are not so imminent that we should skip contemplative cognition and make big mistakes as a result.

The United States' battleship Maine sailed into Havana Harbor on January 25, 1898. At the time, Cubans were rebelling against a Spain which considered Cuba its colony. Some say the Americans were there to show support for the native Cuban bid for freedom.

On the evening of February 15, 1898 the Maine exploded, killing 266 American sailors. The press, with possible nudges from private and government sources, screamed bloody murder. Spain was fingered as the perpetrator. Calls for revenge rang in the streets.

Randolph Hearst, publisher of the New York Journal and other press, wrote headlines insisting that we "Remember the Maine!" "The Spanish", Hearst blustered, "blew up the USS Maine battleship in Havana Harbor." The *Journal* even published artists' drawings showing the Spanish attaching bombs to the underside of the ship. This story helped Hearst sell a lot of newspapers.

An Act of War screamed the headlines of Hearst's papers. Overnight, Spain became the Common Enemy of America and all other peace-loving people. America went to war against Spain between April and August of 1898. Not surprisingly, America beat Spain and took its properties and colonies around the world. Not a bad haul for a five-month war.

We now know from the science of marine archaeology that the USS Maine probably exploded when coal dust spontaneously ignited, blowing the Maine to bits.

Unfortunately for Spain, the explosion of the Maine allowed an American newspaperman to declare Spain a Common Enemy. Ethically, the United States could now *strike them back* (because good people never strike first) and seize Spain's global properties.

Whenever others push us to join a cause against a Common Enemy, we must access the motives of the clarion crier. With speedy responses come thoughtless reactions that might cause more harm than good.

Before we join a lynch mob out for the blood of a Common Enemy, we must ask whether available legal processes can enforce the right or fend off the wrong. We must also access the nature of our Common Enemy's provocation and fashion only a proportionate response. We should ask whether the suspect is really a Common Enemy.

We all understand the Bandwagon effect. Everyone wants to

jump onto the bandwagon, to be part of the scene, to be with the in-group. Who would go against the stream of public will? Who has the courage to stand up to the group and suggest that we "wait a minute"? Knowing that Common Enemies make us dumb and susceptible to the Bandwagon effect, we may be best protected by individuals making a cognitive assessment of the alleged Common Enemy and by daring to say, "Stop, let's think." This may be our duty as citizens.

As we make alliances, we must expect that the enemies of our new allies will now become our Common Enemies.

Exodus 23:22 recognizes this responsibility, "I will be an enemy to your enemies and will oppose those who oppose you."

Putting it another way, the Chinese Communist leader Mao Tse-tung said that, "We shall support whatever the enemy opposes, and oppose whatever the enemy supports." The promise of opposites is Yin and Yang.

With commitments such as these, alliances clearly come with consequences. For this reason alone, we should be cautious about entering alliances, as the cost may be very high.

We must also recognize that humans can fight only so many Common Enemies at one time because our emotional and financial resources are finite. To spend resources fighting a fourth or fifth level Common Enemy is not only wasteful, it might also endanger us.

We must prioritize our Common Enemies. Which is a first level threat? To waste emotional and financial assets containing or fighting a low level Common Enemy may reduce our capacity to fight a first level Common Enemy we have underestimated, not yet recognized or not yet engaged.

In early 1900s America, demon rum was declared a Common Enemy. Universal "Prohibition" resulted. Countless dollars and lives were lost fighting this median level Common Enemy. This Common Enemy was not a threat to everyone, although it was a demon to be fought by certain individuals. By targeting all citizens, this "Prohibition" war wasted resources and fueled the development of organized crime in America. In retrospect, most Americans would now agree that this "Common Enemy" should have been left alone. Learning from the alcohol wars of yesterday, many countries are now dropping their hot wars against soft drugs like marijuana, as being too costly and too futile. Also lost are too many potential tax dollars that may be collected from the monetization of human vice.

Sudden attacks make sudden Common Enemies. Shock, fear and lack of historical Common Enemy experience with a new attacking Common Enemy creates great opportunity for group error. Here, the risks are acting too slowly or too fast.

Before September 11, 2001, few Americans had heard of Bin Laden or his group, Al-Qaeda. Immediately after 9/11, Americans lashed out at Bin Laden, Al-Qaeda and radical Islam. Ready to give their all, these blinded Americans willingly gave up their own civil liberties (allowed themselves to be wiretapped), tortured prisoners and cheered passage of the now infamous USA Patriot Act of 2001.

America's leaders used the confusion and emotion of the time to link Al-Qaeda, the 9/11 perpetrators, with Iraqi President Saddam Hussein and ultimately declared America's first pre-emptive war, against an Iraq that had nothing to do with 9/11. These American leaders had the full support of the majority when they did this deed. Common Enemies have the potential to make us stupid and blind. The stupid and blind can then be led out onto thin ice.

Fear is the first response to a sudden Common Enemy. Do we remember when we first saw a snake slithering at our feet? Thinking back on that experience still gives us a shiver.

The fear is amplified when the *sudden* Common Enemy is also a *new Common Enemy*. Where everything is unknown, there is no past history to predict the risk a new Common Enemy poses. Extra care and time should be spent, whenever possible, in responding to these new Common Enemies.

Common Enemies posing both sudden and new threats stimulate even greater fear that can spread like lightning through a tribe, state or nation. Plagues or threats of weapons of mass destruction can stimulate massive and sometimes out of proportion responses. Indeed, out of proportion responses are more likely to occur when the new Common Enemy is more than a threat and appears to be attacking.

When considering Common Enemies, we should always ask the old question: What came first, the chicken or the egg?

Does conflict follow the pre-existence of a Common Enemy relationship between two or more groups? No doubt this is sometimes the case. But sometimes the victim, or group target-ed by a Common Enemy, doesn't know a Common Enemy is out there until the first attack. Until the Pearl Harbor attack by Japan, most Americans didn't consider Japan to be America's Common Enemy. The average citizen probably didn't give Japan a thought. Within hours of that attack, all Americans united for war against this new and sudden Common Enemy, Japan.

When we suddenly unite against a new Common Enemy, the risks of mob irresponsibility pop up. To avoid these foreseeable risks, each of us must think individually on the issues and facts, even as we are drawn by centripetal force into the core of the uniting group. Avoiding the rush, putting on the brakes, gives us time to think about what we should do in response to our new and sudden Common Enemy.

As we think about a new and sudden Common Enemy, we should each declare our willingness to step forward from the crowd to lead or least yell "Stop!" if the crowd moves toward a cliff. Not all attacks will be as clear-cut as Japan's attack on Pearl Harbor. The dangers of mindless mob behavior are so real in the face of a new and sudden Common Enemy, we should gameplay possible scenarios before such a Common Enemy emerges, to train ourselves to avoid the traps and help our fellow citizens avoid these traps, too.

In addition to training, studying how humans have responded to Common Enemies in the past gives us useful information even if the next Common Enemy we confront is new and sudden.

The military establishments of every country study and train to respond to all kinds of Common Enemies. But this does not relieve us of our individual responsibility to think and act appropriately.

For this reason, each of us should be willing and able to help our civilian leaders make only appropriate and proportionate responses to Common Enemies. And we can only hope our military leaders understand the powers and risks inherent in Common Enemies and their interactions.

In addition to the Common Enemy issues discussed so far, we must also consider that we might want to exploit a Common Enemy for personal or provincial group gain. For example, do we know of office managers who have unified their staff by silently declaring that the big boss is mean, evil and to be feared, and that all us others must band together for survival against this Common Enemy? Certainly we've all heard of the Mutt and Jeff tactics (good guy – bad guy) that cause the criminal to spill the beans to the "good guy" cop to whom they have bonded and avoid the danger and fear engendered by the "bad guy" cop. To the criminal, the "bad guy" cop is the Common Enemy. Regardless, the cops get their criminal confession, and the crafty office manager unites the staff as they both make use of Common Enemies in their day-to-day lives.

Most of us exploiting Common Enemies do so at a low level. The office manager, or the cop using a Common Enemy to get a confession, won't use Common Enemies to start a world war. Regardless, over time, we have seen Common Enemies misused by Otto von Bismarck and Adolf Hitler to take power and to start two world wars. We have also seen the genocides of Jews, Armenians, American Indians and others because we came to view them as Common Enemies or allowed others to scapegoat them as such.

In 2009, newly elected United States President Barack Obama promised to push for health care reform that had eluded United States' presidents from Truman to Clinton. During his first six months on the job, President Obama asked all of the stakeholders to talk, compromise and come forward with a bi-partisan plan. Obama waited and waited.

In September, 2009, things stalled. The negative TV and press ads sponsored by health insurance companies caused an anti-reform tidal wave. In spite of the health insurance companies, most of the other former "say no" stakeholders, like big Pharma and the AMA came out in support of many of Obama's healthcare concepts.

As both strategy and tactic, that was the time for President Obama and supporters of healthcare reform to declare to America that for-profit health insurance companies were the Common Enemies of common Americans. To implement some form of national health insurance, he and reform supporters mobilized the people against insurance companies making 150% profit increases during the worst economic recession in 80 years. The call for Americans to unite against this Common Enemy industry was an effective technique in achieving the goal of health care reform.

To counter, the health insurers and their political surrogates blamed high healthcare costs on trial lawyers and their medical malpractice suits. Lawyers always make good Common Enemies, and this Common Enemy was a good distraction.

Obama created fear worse than the fear created by the lies of the health insurance companies. He united his citizens and led them in battle against the private health insurers that made their profits by accepting premiums and denying coverage and by accepting only healthy people, while refusing to insure or offering expensive limited coverage plans to citizens with pre-existing conditions. These insurance companies were labeled a Common Enemy.

Sometimes citizens want their leaders to use the power of Common Enemies, but the leaders urge caution. Maybe Common Enemies, like pistols, should only be drawn when there is no other choice. Health care reform offered no other choice.

At this point in the book, it might be interesting to predict future Common Enemies.

We know from the past, that old Common Enemies can be recycled. Therefore, Jews, Arabs, Americans, immigrants and other classical Common Enemies can be presented as new Common Enemies forever to future generations.

We also know that new diseases will appear, either from some forbidden land or planet, or morph anew from some old bacteria or virus.

We know that astronomic bodies like asteroids, comets and meteors not yet named, may one day extinguish our species before we even recognize the presence of such a Common Enemy. Maybe we should spend more money to watch what's happening in space?

We know that human nature and our hardwired circuits will cause humans to become Common Enemies to other humans. There are many new wars ahead in our future.

We know that we have Common Enemies within us. Whether called the seven deadly sins, such defects, both hardwired and learned, predict that humans will generate and fight new Common Enemies in perpetuity.

Future Common Enemies will flow from new technologies. As nuclear waste is a Common Enemy by-product of electrical generation from nuclear plants, we can predict that other newer technologies will create new Common Enemies.

Take space junk for example. Since the Soviet Union launched Sputnik into earth orbit in 1957, thousands of satellites, rockets, boosters, stations and other hardware have been launched into space by a number of countries. As a result, the once natural world of space has now become cluttered with space junk. Millions of tiny and large pieces of metal and plastic circle the earth in both low and high space orbit. Some of it is harmlessly vaporized as it enters the earth's atmosphere. Some of it isn't.

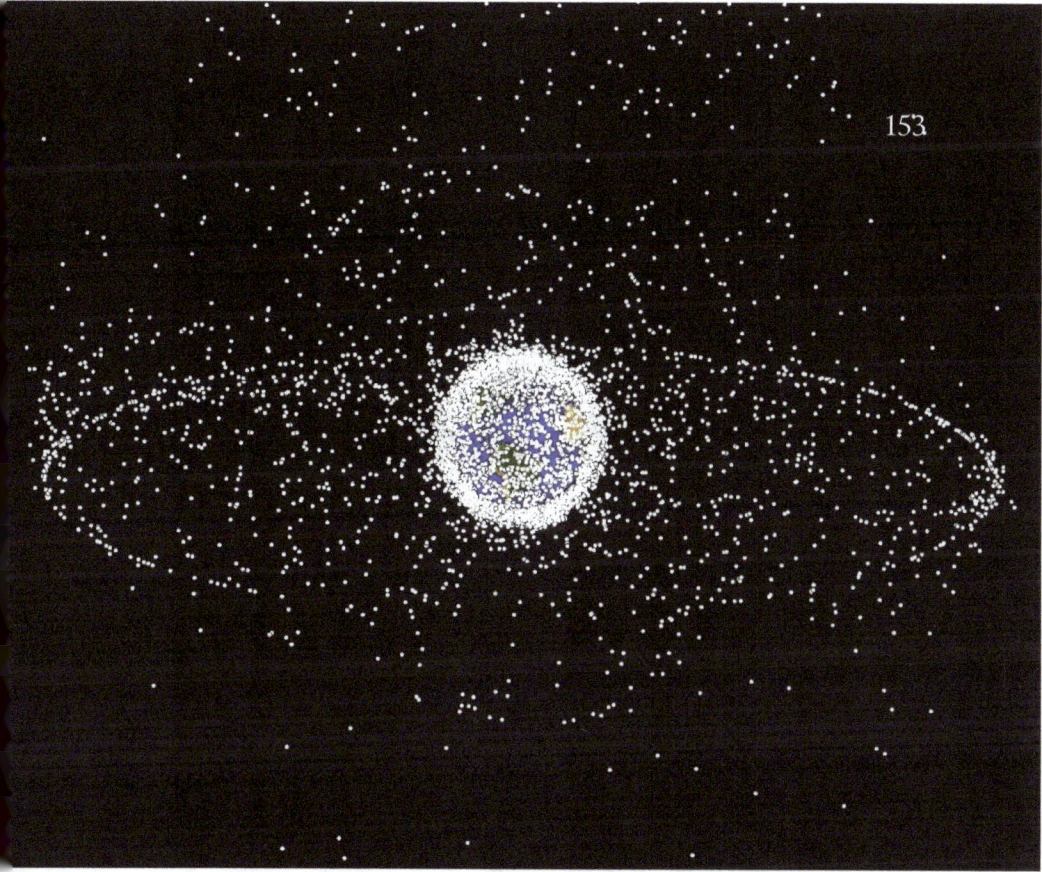

Space junk is man-made orbiting debris from 68 years of human space exploration and use. From little nuts and bolts, the objects are as large as spent rocket booster stages the size of a school bus. From the October 4, 1957 Sputnik launch up to January, 2023 over 55,000 satellites were launched, and today 31,150 of these satellites are space junk. Each is a missile, large and small, that increasingly threatens us and our property on land and in space. This photograph is from a NASA debris plot taken February 1, 2005. Will space junk become a Common Enemy? Photograph courtesy of Wikimedia Commons.

Some objects are big enough or tough enough to come down to hit the earth. Other junk remains in space and poses a threat to useful space objects and to people who are working and living in space.

Space junk, the result of technological advance, and other human-generated wastes, will probably be a source of future Common Enemies.

Slow to be believed Common Enemies, like global warming, now rebranded as "climate change", will grow in scope and intensity. What is now vaguely recognized as a Common Enemy by many, somewhere off in the future, will become an imminent Common Enemy as global warming becomes less theoretical and more real. As they say, nothing focuses a prisoner's mind like a hanging in the morning.

It might be an interesting game to predict and argue for and against possible future Common Enemies.

Hopefully this short book will stimulate thought and scrutiny of the important roles and dangers real and false Common Enemies can pose to nations, groups and individuals. Although most people have an intuitive sense that Common Enemies exert powerful forces over us, little has been written on the subject. Less has been written on their uses and abuses. As computers shrink the world and speed up time, the need to understand the power of Common Enemies becomes even more significant. Common Enemies can appear faster and cause harm sooner almost anywhere in the world. Who knows what damage a lurking Common Enemy can cause with a simple, well-targeted computer virus. We must be vigilant. This is especially true as our priests, rabbis and mullahs remind us we have Common Enemies within us; the BBC, CNN, Al Jazeera and FOX news tell us we have Common Enemies all around us. It's a jungle out there.

Bibliography

Books

Hannah Arendt, The Portable Hannah Arendt, ed, Peter Baehr, Penguin Classics (2003).

W. H. Auden, "Squares and Oblongs", Poets at Work, ed, Charles Abbott, Harcourt Brace Jovanovich (1948).

David P. Barash, Beloved Enemies, Prometheus Books (1994).

Rachel Kahn Best, Common Enemies (Disease Campaigns in America), Oxford University Press (2019).

Contemporary Psychological Research on Social Dilemmas, eds, Ramzi Suleiman, David Budescu, Ilan Fischer, David Messick, Cambridge University Press (2004).

Charles Darwin, Origin of the Species, Random House, (1995).

Frans de Waal, Good Natured: the Origins of Right and Wrong in Humans and Other Animals, Harvard University Press (1997).

Lee Alan Dugalkin, Cooperation Among Animals (An Evolutionary Perspective), Oxford University Press (1997).

Ioannis Evrigenis, Fear of Enemies and Collective Action, Cambridge University Press (2009).

Dan Gardner, The Science of Fear, Plume (2009).

Rene Girard, The Scapegoat, Johns Hopkins University Press (1986).

Jane Goodall, The Chimpanzees of Gombe: Patterns of Behavior, Belknap Press of Harvard University Press (1986)

Montserrat Guibernau, The Identity of Nations, ISBN 07456 26629, Pub. Polity (2008).

G.W.F. Hegel, Elements of the Philosophy of Right, (1821), Oxford University Press (1967).

Thomas Hobbes, Leviathan, OXFORD, at the Clarendon Press, (1965 reprint of 1651 Edition).

Peter Kropotkin, Mutual Aid, ed, Paul Avrich, New York University Press (1972).

Wei Liao-tzu, Tactical Balance of Power, The Seven Military Classics of Ancient China, Ralph D. Sawyer, Westview Press (1993).

John Locke, Second Treatise of Civil Government, ed, C.B. Macpherson, Hacket Publishing (1980).

Niccolo Machiavelli, The Prince, The New American Library (1952).

Allan B. Magruder, John Marshall, Houghton, Mifflin and Company (1885).

Wilbert McKeachie and Charlotte Doyle, Psychology, Addison-Wesley Publishing (1966).

Robert Peckham, Fear: An Alternative History of the World, Profile Books (2023).

Jean-Paul Sartre, The Devil and the Good Lord, Gallimard (1951).

B.F. Skinner, Science and Human Behavior, The Free Press, New York (1965).

David E. Stannard, American Holocaust, Oxford University Press (1993).

The Psychology of Hate, ed, Robert J. Steinberg, American Psychological Association (2004).

U.S. Army Field Manual, Human Intelligence Collector, Operation Approach Techniques and Termination Strategies, FM 2-22.3 (FM34-52): September 6, 2006.

Articles

David Allison, et. al., <u>Annual Deaths Attributable to Obesity in the United States</u>, JAMA, 282, 1530-38 1999.

Tomasz K. Baumiller and Forest J. Gahn, <u>Testing Predator-Driven Evolution with Paleozoic Grinoid Arm Regeneration</u>, Science, Vol. 305, No. 5689,3 September, 2004.

Joel S. Brown and Thomas L. Vincent, <u>Organization of Predator-Prey Communities as an Evolutionary Game</u>, Evolution, Vol. 46, No. 5, October, 1992.

<u>Border controls, Get off the fence</u>, The Economist, pg. 49, March 2, 2024

William J. Cromie, <u>Researchers Find a Gene For Fear</u>, The Harvard Gazette, December 1, 2005.

Bobby Ghosh, <u>How to Make Terrorists Talk</u>, Time, 41, June 8, 2009.

Mark H. Lund, <u>Prehuman Genocide, Human Evolution</u>, Springer Netherlands, Vol. 10:3, July, 1995.

Paul Marrow, Ull Dieckmann and Richard Law, Evolutionary Dynamics of Predator-Prey Systems: an Ecological Perspective, Journal of Mathematical Biology, Vol. 34, Nos. 5-6, May, 1996.

Douglas W. Morris, Enemies of Biodiversity, Carr.J.Zool. Vol. 83, 2005.

Carl Sagan, The Common Enemy, Parade, February 7, 1988.

David Sanger, The World: Russia, China and the U.S.: In Terror, At Last a Common Enemy for the Big Three, New York Times, Sec. 4, pg. 1, October 28, 2001.

Jonathan Steele and Roy McCarthy, Shia and Suni Unite Against a Common Enemy, the U.S. Occupation, The Guardian, Saturday, April 10, 2004.

Thierry Steimer, The Biology of Fear and Anxiety Related Behaviors, Dialogues Clin Neurosci, 4(3), 231-249, September, 2002.

Tobacco Related Mortality in the U.S., MMWR 2008:57(45) 1226-1228.

Vamuk Volkan, The Need to Have Enemies and Allies: A Developmental Approach, Political Psychology, Vol. 6, No. 2, 1985.

Lois Wingerson, Dark History of the White Death, Archaeology, Vol. 62, No. 5, September/October, 2009.

Internet

Ben Kiernan, <u>Holocaust and the United Nations Discussion</u>, Paper Series, Discussion Paper #3, UN Website.

J.K. Ellis, <u>Using Mind Control On a Mob Mentality, Search Wrap. com,</u> July, 2006.

<u>Gale Encyclopedia of Psychology</u>, 2nd ed, Gale Group, 2001.

<u>Types of Advertising Appeals</u>, Buzzle.com

Index

About the Author

John Douglas Peters is a retired attorney whose 40-year career focused on class action and complex litigations. He was an Adjunct Assistant Professor of Law and Medicine at the University of Toledo College of Law and an Adjunct Associate Professor of Medicine at the College of Medicine, Wayne State University. He has authored and co-authored books on law and medicine, art, and rock and roll.